Changes: A Memoir

Changes: A Memoir

A. Gamziukas, M.D.

To Bev ē Best wishes

Al Gamziukas

(mayor of Lakewood curve)

To Helaine

Prologue

The idea of writing this book was suggested by the wife of a friend, but the actual undertaking began at the urging of Helaine, my wife, who was fairly familiar with my past. She was aware of the tremendous effect the events of the thirties and forties had on my family. My experience of constantly moving from one locale to another, of being exposed to many different schools and peer groups, and of being exposed to diametrically opposed political ideologies at a very young age were things she thought made an interesting story that needed to be shared with others.

These memoirs were not written to describe the transit through life of an individual. An individual of no particular note, let alone prominence. Rather, they were created to describe the microcosm of millions of refugees who, through the agendas of great powers, lost everything, including their birthright. Numbering in the millions, they were consigned to DP camps, mainly in Germany, and were, eventually, given only one viable choice -- to emigrate. All they wanted was to return home, but to most of them that meant either death or exile in Siberia at the hands of NKVD.

Essentially, this memoir follows the experience of a young boy as he leaves his own stream to enter the much larger river of the west. As he grows up, we witness his transformation to a physician in his chosen new society.

Chapter One

The sun was already high above the dunes and pines of Palanga. It was just one week after the summer solstice. Seven a.m. in a Lithuanian summer seems almost like midmorning. This day was rather cool.

The breeze off the Baltic did not make it any warmer. I was out there with my two granddaughters, Jordan and Lydia, teaching them how to gather small pieces of amber in the sand after the waves receded. Few other amber pickers were there. The cool breeze kept the other tourists either in bed or having breakfast in one of Palanga's many coffee shops. The beach would not become crowded until close to noon, at which point, presumably, the temperature would be friendlier.

This exercise took me back to the halcyon days of the middle and late thirties. It was a time of peace between the great wars. My world consisted of Kaunas, Sirviai, and Palanga. I gathered amber on the beach, learned to swim in the sea, and picked mushrooms in Grandfather's forest near Sirviai.

My earliest memory is that of an apartment on Visinskio Street in 1935 or 1936. Strangely, I can only recall the day we were moving from it to a yellow four-unit dwelling on Gedraiciu Street, just around the corner. This new apartment was rather modest. It had only a kitchen, bathroom, father's study, dining room, and a large bedroom.

Near both places was a huge pond. In the summertime not much happened in it. I never saw anyone fishing or swimming. By November, however, it froze solid and became a huge skating rink. Lights illuminated it in the evening, loudspeakers played dance music, numerous vendors sold hot chocolate, and the ice was covered with crowds of skaters. Kids did their thing while young couples skated to the music. Many an older pair glided hand in hand, probably reminiscing about days gone by.

1n 1992 Helaine and I walked past the house on Gedraiciu Street. It was still as yellow as it was when my family took up residence in it. The paint was cracked, but it continued to adhere to the clap boards. The paint seemed to be an indelible memorial to a very distant past.

Across the hall lived a family that moved to Brazil very soon after our arrival. The head of the family, a distinguished looking gentleman, was an employee of the Ministry of Foreign affairs. Apparently, he was sent to occupy some diplomatic post.

Soon after their departure, the apartment was occupied by a Jewish couple. The new tenants held regular meetings with some people we did not know. These gatherings took place several times a month and were concluded with a song that had a beautiful melody. Although I could not make out the words, I knew the language was Russian. Mother told me the song was called "Internationale". Several years later I discovered this was the anthem of the World Communist Party. This was my first introduction to what later became the Communist holocaust.

In the summer Mother and I stayed on my grandparent's farm for weeks at a time. Grandmother Olga, my maternal grandmother, was Russian. Her father was a general in the Czar's army until he was murdered by the

Bolsheviks during the October revolution. She met Grandfather while he was studying law at the University of St. Petersburg, converted to Catholicism, and married him. It was because of her that I became fluent in Russian.

Mother was born in Russia in 1906. During the great upheaval, which later became known as the Communist Revolution, they left by horse for Lithuania. I have always felt Grandmother had a very unhappy life there. She spoke limited Lithuanian and spent all of her time in Sirviai managing the estate. I don't think she got to bask in the limelight of Grandfather's career.

Grandmother's great avocation was floriculture. Her English garden in Sirviai was remarkable. Her giant dahlias had no equal. Even the dahlias on the island of Mainau in Lake Constance paled by comparison. Here is where I became familiar with the names of the flowers and the amount of work that went into developing and maintaining this beautiful corner of the farmstead. Grandmother worked at every aspect with the help of several maids. The design, color distribution, and bloom, however, were done only by her.

I recall Mother telling me about their journey from St Petersburg. They were doing all they could to reach Lithuanian lines. They knew the Baltics had risen up against both the Russians and the remnants of the withdrawing, defeated Germans.

Her most memorable tale was of crossing the river Dauguva, also known as the Western Dvina. It was very late winter. The river ice was already melting and covered by a substantial amount of water. The bridges were not available as they were either destroyed or patrolled by armed groups. These groups were known to shoot first and ask questions later. Rather characteristic behavior of unsettled times. Well, the horses managed to get my family's half-submerged sleigh across the river without breaking though the ice.

Shortly afterwards they reached Sirviai, a typical central Lithuanian village situated 41 kilometers northeast of Kaunas, on the eastern slope of a small hill. The village could not be seen from the west until one reached the top of that hill. It consisted of several dozen thatched-roof farm buildings and had a population of fifty to sixty people.

My grandfather's farm was initially acquired by the Boreisa family in 1854. I found the deed among Mother's papers after her death. The documents stated that my great, great, great mother's name was Darata. That was a mystery. Looking for answers, I talked to an old Lithuanian friend. Initially, he couldn't answer my questions. He called his brother in Hamilton, Ontario. His brother, at that time, was about 100 years old! He immediately answered that her name was "Dorothy". So me and mine can trace our family, at least on one side, to the mid 19th century. How many people, unless they are nobility of some sort, know their grandmother's name so many generations back?

My grandfather, Julian Boreisa, was born in the village in 1882. He was the oldest of three children. His brother Joseph was a few years younger and Sister Veronica was the youngest. While Grandfather was studying in St Petersburg, Joseph ran away from home. He left for America without his parent's permission. There he changed his name to Brazer and married a Polish woman, apparently from Cleveland. If memory serves me correctly, he lived in St. Louis, Missouri.; Cleveland, Ohio; Utica, New York; and Medina, New York before eventually settling in Buffalo. I never really understood why he changed a short Lithuanian name. The new moniker made Joe Boreisa seem to be a Scot!

But those were different times. In America non Anglo-Saxon names were allegedly a negative, even in the late fifties. At that time I was in Buffalo, working as a pharmacist during my last year of medical school. A local M.D. asked me, "What are you going to do with that handle if you want to be successful?" Not wanting to tell him right then and there what he could do with his inquiry, I tactfully replied that I would give it some thought. The man was very helpful in other ways. For example, when he discovered I could not afford a microscope he gave me his to use for an entire year.

The neighborhood he hailed from, and where I eventually practiced, consisted of almost equal parts Polish, Italian (mainland), German, and Irish, with a sprinkling of Russians. In east Buffalo colloquial, one would say the Lovejoy area was a second-generation immigrant town made up of "pollacks", "wops", "krauts", and "micks". Only a very small percentage of these people changed their names to fit in. Explanations for this willing ethnic metamorphosis ranged from "the name was very long" to "you had to have an American name to get a job". My final decision was that I neither wanted, nor needed, to become an "Anglo-Saxon".

Grandfather's sister Veronica married a well-to-do farmer by the name of Adolfas Gradauskas. Her new husband owned a substantial farm on the other side of the Didenai forest. Going through the woods, their farm was about a one-hour's walk from Sirviai. The buildings were located on the edge of a gully through which ran a small creek, the Paberze, that gave the entire area an idyllic appearance. The farm took its name from the creek. The Gradauskases had no children and died at Paberze during the Russian occupation. Mother corresponded with her Aunt Veronica for many years, but I know neither the time of the Gradauskases' death nor when their correspondence ceased. An attaché case of old photographs, which belonged to Mother, contains pictures of what I think are Veronica and her husband.

Grandfather, on returning from Russia, got a job with the local court system. His first position was that of court interrogator. My guess is this was a job supervising police interrogations. I don't think Grandpa ever used a rubber hose as a persuader. This position was much lower than that of a *procurator* (prosecutor). His career gradually developed as he began to climb the ladder of achievement and success within the Lithuanian Ministry of Justice.

He acquired his property, family homestead, and land by buying Veronica's and Joseph's shares in the estate. The land became Boreisa property in the mid-nineteenth century. The deed indicates that forests and additional arable plots were purchased up until the early nineteen-twenties. By now the farm reached its final size of about eighty hectares.

At this point, Grandfather bought out Veronica's and Joseph's shares of the estate. On this occasion his brother Joseph, now with the last name of Brazer, returned from the States for the transaction. This was his only visit to Lithuania and the last time he saw his brother and sister, as well as Sirviai, where he was born. Of course, one must realize that 747s were not flying over the Atlantic in those days.

Mother once told me about a transatlantic telephone conversation between Grandfather and his brother. The time of the call was set by previous correspondence. Once the call was placed it took several hours to get through. A mutually agreed upon time precluded the possibility that Brother Joseph would not be available. I wonder how much such a call cost.

In the early thirties, Grandfather was appointed a Justice of the Supreme Court of the Republic of Lithuania. This Court, unlike its American counterpart, consisted of three Justices. The appointments were made by President Antanas Smetona, leader of the then-ruling Nationalist party. Grandfather, however, eschewed all political parties and political activity. He was later awarded two high medals for his performance as a Justice. It was the same A. Smetona who hung these medals on Grandfather's neck. It appears that in those days Lithuania expected its judges to remain apolitical. Politicians, even ecclesiastic high brass, knew they had no influence with the judiciary.

In 1932, soon after Grandfather's appointment to the High Bench, my parents were married. Both graduated that year from the law school of Vytautas

Magnus University in Kaunas. A montage picture of the class shows their photographs next to each other. They lived just around the corner from Grandmother Gamziukas.

I was born on Sunday, October 30, 1933, at the Red Cross Hospital in Kaunas.

In 1992 I went to see the hospital. The building in which I had been born was now dwarfed by the modern Kaunas medical school complex. The old front door was still there and functional. It probably served as a back entrance even though it opened onto Laisves Aleja (Liberty Alley). "Alley" isn't an accurate description as Laisves Aleja is truly a magnificent boulevard.

During the late thirties, my Mother (Valerija) and I spent a good part of each summer in Sirviai. The rest of the summer was spent in Palanga, where my father (Peter Gamziukas) rented an apartment when he took his annual vacation. My father was an attorney who worked at the Ministry of Finance in Kaunas. Even as a junior attorney he got a one-month vacation, as was customary in those days. To this day I don't know which was more fun, the farm or the sea. I looked forward to both with great anticipation.

The Gamziukas clan was from southwestern Lithuania. Father was born in a town called Sartininkai. The town is located near what used to be the border of East Prussia. That part of Lithuania was interesting in that many people were bilingual and it had many Lutheran churches. This was due to the proximity of Germany's easternmost province. That was the place where the panzers started to roll north when Hitler attacked Russia in 1941.

My paternal Grandfather was a civil servant in the Czar's customs service. He moved his family many times. At one time they even lived in Russia, in the town of Velikije Luky. One of my younger uncles took a trip to that area during the Russian occupation. He found people with our name, but could not establish their relationship to us. Gamziukas is not that common a name and its linguistic history is not very flattering. A book dealing with the meaning of Lithuanian names defines Gamziukas as "an unkempt or shabby person."

Spending summers on the farm gave me a tremendous opportunity to see nature up close. I saw pigs farrowing, cow's calving, and the sowing and harvesting of various fruits and vegetables. I recall very well those early summer days when one particular glade in Grandfather's forest became red with wild strawberries. My friends and I would sit in the red meadow and eat until our stomachs were full. No cultivated strawberry could compete with the wild ones in flavor, taste, or aroma.

Towards late summer, mushroom season arrived with its horn of cornucopia. One had to be careful when picking wild mushrooms. Some were poisonous to eat. Some could make one sick or even be fatal. However, we had no problems. Our picking principle was simple. Pick only those one knew to be edible. As an additional precaution, my basket was always carefully gone over by one of the kitchen maids when I returned to the farm.

The king of the mushrooms is a boletus species the Lithuanian's call baravykas. In Germany it is known as Steinpilz, and in Italy, porcino. The woods were also full of chanterelles and other mushroom varieties. What passes for a supermarket mushroom in America would probably be considered high-grade swill in Sirviai. Years later, however, I was surprised to find out that the finest boletus in the world grow in the state of Colorado. Their size attracts many affluent mushroom pickers from Lithuania.

One day in early summer, we younger kids joined some older boys on an interesting hunting-picnic expedition into Grandfather's woods. Everyone had a sling shot. Onions, potatoes, and a small slab of bacon were the rest of our supplies for the day. The older boys found a tree containing multiple nests of striped doves. The older boys had us surround it. On their command, everyone fired their slingshots into the tree. This resulted in several downed pigeons. We repeated this several times in other parts of the forest until we had enough birds to feed us. A fire was started. A skillet was used to render the bacon, and then to fry the potatoes and onions. Then the doves were plucked, cleaned, properly cut up, and fried in the lard. The resulting feast was indescribably delicious. Since that time, I have eaten many varieties of game birds that have been prepared using many different recipes. Nothing has ever come close to that meal in Grandfather's forest.

When I was very young, Grandfather taught me horseback riding and later, at about age nine, to drive a team of horses. From the very beginning he emphasized that if you give the horse the idea that you're afraid or unsure of yourself you will not be able to impress upon the animal that you are the boss.

My first experience with a team and a loaded cart was during the potato harvest in 1943. A wagon had been loaded with many sacks of potatoes and there was no one to drive. Other teams had already left the fields for the farm, and the remaining workers were hurrying to fill another load as the sun was already below the steeple top of Zeimiai church. Grandfather rode by on a horse and quickly solved the problem. He told me to take the team and the loaded cart to the village. I suppose this was the equivalent of a father handing the car keys to his son for the first time.

The trip went uneventfully and no one made any remarks. It must have looked very natural in the country to see a nine year old kid drive a team of horses. No one gave me any formal lessons or taught how to do it. It was through repeated observation that I was able to accomplish this.

As fate would have it, this was the first and last time that I drove a team. The following spring there was no such opportunity. And by that summer the family would be beyond the borders of Lithuania, deep within what was then called "Greater Germany".

Village friends were my daily companions. We took excursions into the woods, swam in nearby gravel pits, and fished for northern pike in Lankesa creek. The first significant fish I ever landed was a nice-sized northern. However, it was not caught with bait and hook; I speared it under a bridge, where the fish congregated because it was cool. I suppose this was not fair, but the fine points of sportsmanship were not in my grasp at this early age.

I remember most days being warm and sunny. Occasionally, a late summer thunderstorm blew the huge poplar tree that grew across the street from our house into a frenzy. However, I really don't recall any long stretches of rainy weather. I suppose every day is warm and sunny when a child feels secure, does things that interest him, and is not burdened by the worries of the adults.

It was in Sirviai that I began my education. A farmer's small house had one room dedicated to education. Thus, it can truly be said that my education commenced in a one room school house. The student body numbered less than ten. It consisted of children of all ages. The teacher was a graduate of teacher seminary and paid by the state. This was his first assignment.

Subsequently, I attended schools in Kaunas and Zeimiai. Although I now don't recall the sequence, I went to a lot of schools because of being displaced by the Russian occupation and the war that followed it. It was difficult learning this way. For instance, Russian civics was taught differently in different schools.

From the conversation of my elders and the occasional radio newscast I learned that September 1939 was the start of World War Two. After Poland was attacked by both Hitler and Stalin, it ceased to exist as a political entity. Lithuania was at this point trying to stay neutral. The eastern part of Lithuania, which had been occupied by the Poland after Pilsudski's unprovoked attack in the early twenties, immediately reverted to Lithuanian control. The Molotov-Ribbentrop pact was already a done deal, but people didn't know the details. They knew there was a Russian/German alliance, but no one knew exactly what was going on.

Father obtained a position as CEO of Patrimpas, a cigarette factory located in Vilnius. He moved there immediately and searched for an apartment for our family. Mother followed one or two weeks later. I was left in the care of my grandparents in both Sirviai and Kaunas. To this day I can only speculate as to the reasons for my being left behind.

One beautiful and sunny afternoon, in the summer of 1940, I was filling a trough located right next to our well. All of a sudden I saw village kids tearing down the street, yelling something about many horse-pulled carts approaching from the north. Like a scared cat, I leaped to the top of the picket fence separating the farmyard from the street. Dust rose from the unpaved road connecting Sirviai with the next village to the north. The size of the dust cloud indicated that it was churned up by many animals and wheels. What could this be?

Before I could come up with a possible answer, the first cart rolled by. Holding the reins was a man in a strange uniform. He wore a cap like that of a Lithuanian air force pilot, but that was where the similarity ended. He had no tunic. Instead, his upper body was covered by a large shirt that was not tucked into his trousers. Around his waist he wore a leather belt with a large metal buckle. A red star, just like the one on his cap, was on the buckle. On the star was a hammer and sickle. His trousers were tucked in dusty boots that covered more than half of his calf. They were a bit shorter than Lithuanian farmer's boots, let alone normal length riding boots. Strung across his back was a very long rifle. The contents of the cart were under a tarp.

Some kind of commander rode by on a rather nice chestnut horse. He rode into the area of the well and started helping himself to the water in the trough. He told those in the carts to use the pond to water the horses. In fluent Russian I told him that the water in the pond at that time of year was avoided, even by the farm animals. He was surprised by my linguistic ability and asked where I had learned Russian. I replied that my Grandmother had taught me.

The convoy took some two hours to drive through the village. We kids had not the slightest idea what was going on. Why was the Russian army here? There were two or three Lithuanian Communists in the township of Zeimiai. They told us the Red Army had come to liberate us. "Why?" we wondered. "From whom?"

That fall, in school, we had the explanation rammed into us in heavy doses. Comrade Stalin was liberating Lithuania from its bourgeois oppressors. Comrade Stalin welcomed Lithuania into the great brotherhood of nations, the Soviet Union, etc., etc. The following autumn we spent much time pasting over pages in our textbook. Pages with nationalistic content like the country's coat of arms, a portrait of the president, and the words of the Lithuanian national anthem. These now represented bourgeois decadence and were forbidden by the communists. Only the arithmetic textbook escaped this vandalism.

Otherwise, except for learning communist songs, days went on in a pretty normal fashion. The teacher, a card-carrying member of the Lithuanian Communist Party, was a very decent sort of a guy. He knew that I came from the village "aristocracy" and that Grandfather was a justice of the "decadent capitalist" supreme tribunal. He warned my parents and Grandparents to never discuss politics and current events in front of me because officials would eventually ask me about the adult conversations at home.

Exactly on my birthday, the thirtieth of October, a car stopped by the farm gate. A Russian major got out and came to the door, supposedly to get directions for a manor located some four kilometers away. His demeanor, elegant appearance, and manicured fingers suggested he was an educated and polished individual. Because it was late afternoon, Grandmother invited him to stay for tea. He was more than delighted to accept the invitation. During this "social affair" I told him that day was my seventh birthday. He made me sit on his lap and asked me "Whom are we going to fight?" I answered quickly. "Germany." He explained that Germany was an ally of the Soviet Union. At that age I knew nothing of the Molotov-Ribbentrop pact. "America," I suggested, "America, to za daliko," he explained. (America is too far). My family members must have all developed an instantaneous cardiac arrhythmia. They were afraid my answer would be "Russia".

The next summer, while in Sirviai, we heard that Father had been arrested in Vilnius and locked up in a Lukiskiu prison. Three individuals from the NKVD had knocked on the door of my parent's apartment at 4:00 AM. They told my father he was to go with them. Mother must have been beside herself during that episode. There were rumors that people were being executed at the prison. Their crimes? Patriotism, being well to do, belonging to a political party, and being a member of the *inteligencia* (the educated class). These were all enemies of the people. The communists never explained what that really meant. I suppose anyone who did not dance to their tune was an enemy of the people.

A few days after his incarceration, Mother decided to find out if Father was still among the living and if he was still in Lukiskiu prison. All her previous inquiries had been rebuffed with noncommittal, vague answers. When she asked about legal representation she was told it would be provided by the state, despite the fact that she was an attorney. She decided to go to the prison under the pretext that she needed Father's signature to resolve some utility problem. She was not allowed to see him, but a NKVD official took the document. Eventually, he returned with father's signature. Father's signature was unique and not easily forged, so Mother knew that he was alive in Lukiskiu prison.

Shortly after this incident, Albertas Tarulis, the husband of my Aunt Nina, phoned Mother and told her my father would be released that same afternoon. How he found out and why Father was released remain mysteries to this day. There was a rumor that a petition by a number of ordinary workers at the cigarette factory had something to do with it.

After this horrendous experience, both my parents came to Sirviai where the family lived until after the arrival of the Germans. The family was together again, and to me a more secure type of existence seemed present. But security was an ephemeral concept in those nightmarish days of the first Russian occupation. Every day brought new evidence of a horrible plague in Lithuania. Fear gripped the country. The question "Are we next?" hung like a black cloud over everyone's head.

One gray summer day, a short-statured Jew, the head of the local Communist party called "Soviet", appeared at the farm and ordered Grandfather to send two twin horse-and-cart teams, along with their drivers, to a point in Kedainiai where the Russians were building a military airport. Grandfather protested that we were in the midst of summer chores which could not be done without the teams the apparatchik was ordering the farm to give up. I was there and heard the little, arrogant bastard explain that the might of the Red Army superseded any kulak's need to further exploit the working man. After the war started the apparachik was caught and turned over to the German SS.

I mention ethnicity because I find it interesting that Jews who were upstanding members of local business or the professional community had nothing to do to with the harassment of the local population by the communist party. As a matter of fact, they also suffered from Bolshevik persecution. It was the never-do-wells, the trash, and other of society's outcasts, both

Lithuanian and Jewish, that felt the glory days were almost within their grasp.

Later that summer there was some sort of communist celebration. It took place at the local manor. We kids had to recite communist poetry written by collaborating Lithuanian "poets". I got up on the stage and started on about Stalin and me going together to the sun and stars. At this point a candidate of the party (you could always tell them by their blue suits and red neckties) started playing an accordion in an attempt to drown my declamation. I, after all, was of the kulak class. The commies that were present had set me up. However, much to their dismay, I continued traveling with Stalin as loud as I could. At the end I got a big round of applause from ordinary Lithuanian farm people. They did not applaud the contents of the poem. To this day I feel they were congratulating my resistance against the red musician.

Around the middle of June, I checked the area of the orchard that was dedicated to berries. There was a multitude of currant, raspberry and gooseberry bushes. I was selecting the most succulent gooseberries when I suddenly heard motor noise. In those days it was a rare phenomenon in Sirviai. Weeks would go by between cars or trucks traversing the village. As the noise approached, I ran to the orchard fence to get closer to the street. A Russian Gas (a replica of an earlier American Ford truck) was approaching. In the back were several women, one of them in a night gown, and one man. I recognized the man as the owner of Gabrielava manor. The group was accompanied by two Russian soldiers holding rifles with fixed bayonets. Russian bayonets were extremely long. Within seconds the truck disappeared in a cloud of dust. Although perplexed, I returned to the berry bushes.

Later that day, I discovered that the truck had been heading for Jonava railway station. At that time I was unaware that I had witnessed the beginning of the Great Deportations. At Jonava, men were separated from women and children, and placed on a different train. Most of these families were never reunited.

That day was the 14th of June, recognized now as a Lithuanian state holiday called the Day of Mourning and Hope. I am sure that leftist revisionist historians will paint that day in different colors, if they haven't already, but their forked-tongue brushes will not erase the memories of what I witnessed. Only after the arrival of the German army did I learn that tens of thousands of Lithuanians were deported to Siberia.

This was the day we started changing our nocturnal location. Word was out in Kaunas that both Boreisa and Peter Gamziukas were on the NKVD list. When an individual was arrested, his family was as well. We spent nights in Trepalava, in Grandfather's forest cottage, and the homes of Father's friends and acquaintances. One night we slept in a field of rye. At that time of year the rye was so tall that no one on the road could see you unless you were standing.

On Sunday, the twenty second of June, while listening to the radio, we heard a well-known radio personality interrupt the program for an important announcement by Molotov, the Commissar of Foreign Affairs. He spoke in Russian and announced that Germany had unexpectedly, in a most cowardly and treacherous way attacked the Soviet Union. He went on to say that Soviet Might would rise up, and the Red Banner would eventually fly over Berlin.

There went the Ribbentrop-Molotov pact! My grandparents and Mother fell to their knees to thank the Almighty for deliverance from the Red Terror. The next day, control of Lithuanian radio was taken over by patriot freedom fighters, and the communist voice went still. The radio began broadcasting local news, as well as instructions for meeting the German army and harassing withdrawing reds. By Friday, German army infantry carriers were in Sirviai.

This change of occupiers was not entirely peaceful. The Village street became choked with the carriages of those withdrawing with the Russians. These included disjointed Red Army stragglers, Lithuanian communists, and local Jews who knew well the danger of living under the now victorious Nazis.

One evening during this time, a son of a Jewish hardware store owner whom Grandfather had been doing business with for many years arrived at our house with his young wife and a newborn infant. We put them up for the night, but in the morning they joined the withdrawing multitudes. A few days later word got back that the son had hung himself, leaving his small family to their own devices.

That same morning, a Russian major was seen riding off on Geisha, my Grandfather's horse. The major was armed. Had he no weapon the farmhands would have gladly made him stay in Lithuania. Six feet under that is.

Later the same morning, Grandfather had the farm people dig a bunker large enough to accommodate everyone on the farm. The bunker was about one-and-a-half meters deep and four by five meters in size. The roof consisted of logs so heavy that only a hitched horse could drag them. They were over five inches thick and flat on opposite sides. Originally, they had been prepared for the building of a new barn.. On top of this log roof about one meter of earth was the final cover. One corner had an opening which served as an entry way. This relatively protective shelter was located under some old apple trees and surrounded by berry bushes that had been slated to be removed. Essentially, the entire contraption was not visible unless one stumbled on it.

The following morning, Luftwaffe planes flew overhead and we all heard artillery in the distance, west of Zeimiai. Our small community started preparing food in case we needed to stay in the bunker for an indeterminate period of time. This consisted mainly of baking many loaves of bread and gathering everything hanging in the smoke house: seasoned sausages, hams, and slabs of bacon. Everything was removed because the smoke chimney was located in the middle of the farm dwelling. If the house caught fire all the smoked goodies would go up with it. All cheeses and butter likewise became part of the bunker pantry. At about noon, sporadic small arms fire drew closer, but Father and Grandmother Olga were having too much fun hard-boiling eggs in the main kitchen to care. They boiled dozens upon dozens of eggs. I don't remember what provisions were made for water. The well was all the way across the farm, near the barns.

Our horses had been turned loose within the farm perimeter fence. In the early afternoon they were grazing about fifty or sixty meters from the bunker. Suddenly, they bolted in all directions. There were leaves falling from the fruit trees near where the animals had been grazing. Why were the leaves falling? It was high summer!

Within a few minutes it became obvious. Machine gun bursts were flying through the tops of the trees. No one knew if they were from the Russians or the Germans. Fortunately, this fire-fight was very brief. In a few minutes all was quiet. After about one hour, some people, including Father and Grandmother Olga, went back to the farm house.

Late that afternoon, the first German scout car arrived at the farm. Father, who was fluent in German, went to talk to an officer. The young lieutenant informed him that our farm would be used as their regimental headquarters. Having no choice in the matter, Father welcomed the Germans to the farm in an effort to create a good first impression. The lieutenant very curtly asked Father where he had learned to speak "educated" German. Father replied, "Gymnasium." Father had no intention of explaining to a junior officer about his business travels to Germany and other western European countries. He informed the German that he wished to speak to his commanding officer immediately. The young lieutenant got the message that Father was much more than an ordinary Lithuanian farmer. He immediately became polite and accommodating. Father knew that Germans understood authority. Doubtless, he was also a good bluffer.

That evening there were half-track personnel carriers, trucks, and "kuebel wagens" parked inside and outside the farm fence. The German field kitchen staff was cooking something salmon-colored that had beans in it. The soldiers were also eating black bread which, in appearance at least, could have been our own farm bread. Some were going for a second helping. They certainly had enough to eat.

Several communication trucks were parked in a distant corner of the orchard. They were the only trucks that sprouted whip antennas. Next to them, above the orchard canopy, very tall radio masts jutted into the sky. They needed guy wires to support them.

One of the trucks was really a van. Through its back door I could see several soldiers wearing radio ear muffs and twisting dials on the large radios in front of them. They had no problem with five boys inspecting the scene.

The German officers wore peaked hats with an eagle and swastika on them. Without exception they all wore side arms on their belts.

The traffic on the only village street was overwhelmingly military. "They have no horses," observed one of my friends. Indeed, it was some time before a slow-moving horse-drawn convoy was seen, hugging the shoulder of the road as it made its way north.

At one point, one of the soldiers asked me something. I did not have the vaguest idea what his question was, but I answered, "ja." Apparently, it was an appropriate response. He asked something again. I again answered, "ja." He hesitated a few seconds and then laughed as he realized that I knew absolutely no German.

The following evening, Grandfather invited the senior regimental officers for dinner at the farmhouse. I was told to stay out of the dining room.

All I recall is being in bed while a spirited conversation in German took place downstairs. My parents and Grandfather were all proficient enough in German to engage in a long conversation over coffee.

We were already living in Buffalo when Father told me the remark the colonel had made as he was saying good bye. "You regard us as liberators and greet us with flowers," he said. "But those that come after us will be very different." Indeed, they were. Arrests and deportations, this time to concentration camps in Germany, soon followed at the hands of the Gestapo.

The regiment soon moved north. Sometimes, even now, I wonder how many of those happy, victorious soldiers ever saw their homes again.

The next day various stories spread through the village. While I was listening to them, the village communal cowherd came and told the men around me that there was a wounded Russian soldier in a nearby rye field. He led the group to the object of his excitement. Indeed, some 150 meters away, at the edge of the rye field, sat a Russian. His left pant leg was bloody from about mid-thigh, and he was holding it to prevent it from moving. Tears streamed down his cheeks. He was so young! In his late teens, I thought.

On seeing us approach, he started to speak. One of the men said, "Get Boreisa's grandson over here. He speaks Russian." And so I came to be standing in front of the soldier. The poor fellow was a sorry sight. His hair was messed up, both of his hands were bloody, and his clothing was dirty and torn. He had no firearms. His canteen was on the ground, obviously empty, and he was asking for water. I translated this message to the others. As a man went to get something for him to drink, the young soldier started pleading, "Don't turn me over to the Germans, please!" One of the villagers observed, "If Lithuanian freedom fighters get to him first, he will wish he had been captured by the German army". I explained to him the need for cleaning up and bandaging. "Tell him he needs a doctor," one of the men said. I did as I was told.

Just then, an army truck appeared out of a cloud of dust. Germans got out and surveyed the situation before lifting the soldier into the back of their vehicle and driving off. Well, our dilemma was solved. The young soldier had become a prisoner of war. Had Lithuanian insurrectionists gotten to him first, he would have been killed on the spot.

Chapter Two

Winters made the greatest impression on my early memories of Kaunas. Trips downtown with Mother left the most vivid memories. Laisves Aleja (Liberty Boulevard) was a variegated world of blinking, moving, and dancing neon lights. The lights came on early because winter sundown in those latitudes happened around four p.m.. The jingling of one-horse sleighs replaced the quiet summertime hacks, though taxis were still very much present. Indeed, going shopping downtown, in the valley of the confluence of the Nemunas and Neris rivers, was a descent into a real winter wonderland.

In foreign literature these two rivers are referred to as Memel or Nieman, and Vilia, respectively.

Kaunas in midwinter could get quite cold; minus 20 degrees Celsius was not unusual. Both the Neris and Nemunas were frozen to the point where wartime traffic would drive over the ice. One of the bridges had been blown up at the beginning of the war, but the locals soon found where it was safe to descend to the river and where it was easiest to ascend the opposite bank

In Lithuania, Christmas is the main religious holiday. With the exception of the Russian occupation, during which Christmas was not allowed to be observed, the holiday had always been celebrated over two days.

Our Christmas was divided between our apartment and both grandparents' houses. Kucios, the Christmas Eve supper, was always at Grandfather Boreisa's. Kucios is a Lithuanian tradition. It consists of a twelve-course cold supper preceded by the breaking of the Christmas wafer. Everyone breaks the wafer with every other member of the family. In really large families this can take up a lot of time. The twelve dishes represent the twelve apostles and are served on a table covered with hay, then with a table cloth. Hay is a reminder that Jesus was laid in the manger. The supper is always meatless and no alcoholic beverages are allowed.

Grandfather's magnificent apartment had a large living room where a Christmas tree reached all the way to the top of the nine-foot high ceiling. I still have pleasant memories of the aroma of the fir tree (never a pine) mixed with that of burning beeswax candles set on its branches.

The tree had to be carefully watched. The naked flame of candles was known to start fires in the homes of the careless. One time our neighbors left their tree unattended while seeing guests to the door. When they returned, the tree was on fire. Fortunately, they did not forget to keep a bucketful of water in the same room.

Presents, oh, the presents, were stacked around the tree. I looked forward with great expectation to opening them. At Grandfather's they were opened after Kucios. The following day we would open more at home. And on the second day of Christmas, at Grandmother Petronele's, still more!

Every summer before the Russian occupation, the family would vacation in Palanga for three or four weeks. Palanga, located on the rather short Lithuanian Baltic coastline, is a summer resort attracting international clientele. Pristine beaches are separated from the town by tall dunes and a narrow pine forest. The town is replete with souvenir stores and upscale stores dealing in silver or gold amber jewelry. Many restaurants of various price ranges cater to tourists who walk the streets in the evening. Near the hill of Birute, the resplendent palace of count Tiskevisius dominates the scene. Today it is one of the top amber museum's in the world. When I visited the resort in 2003, I noticed Swiss, French, and German license plates alongside local, Russian and Polish ones. Palanga now also has an international airport.

Father joined us on weekends, sometimes staying for a full week. Rooms were rented in one of our few favored villas and the beach vacation would begin.

Before Father bought a used Renault, we took the train. The trip, short by international distance standards, lasted all morning. Driving from Kaunas to Palanga, however, would have been no quicker. While today there is a modern expressway with an 80 mph speed limit, in the thirties we traveled on roads that were not macadamized. The average speed was much, much lower than today's speed on the expressway. The driver also had to know where the filling stations were as they weren't marked on a map.

I recall one trip that took almost an entire day. On that particular trip we had a flat. Father changed to the spare. Then the problem was to find a place that would fix the inner tube and vulcanize the tire. We managed to get to Palanga the same day, but after sundown.

I was not fond of the trains. I particularly disliked the recently acquired, very noisy, huge Skoda locomotives.

While on vacation we spent the day by the sea until "high-tea" time. At this time adults at the villa would be served tea and crumpets, English style. We kids would get milk and buns. I was never very fond of milk, but during these high teas it was unavoidable.

The Baltic Sea beach is truly magnificent. The sand is very fine, and the shallow sea bottom extends very far, perhaps a hundred meters, before it becomes deep. An ideal beach for kids and non-swimmers.

Amber washes up on the shore all day long. The average size would only be that of a small pebble; however, one of my uncles found a piece the size of a human fist while walking along the shore in early morning after a night storm.

It was in Palanga that Father and his friends taught me to swim. It seemed so easy. I wondered why everyone could not swim. Both of my parents were excellent swimmers.

That very evening, the family walked out on the sea-pier, which was very similar to the one in Naples, Florida. There was a motor boat ride in the launches that took tourists out to sea. While we waited our turn to walk down the stairs, I managed to tumble off the pier into the sea. Mother became extremely upset as she had not been told about my recently acquired swimming ability. I swam near one of the boats and was fished out within minutes. At that time I wondered why there was so much excitement on the pier. Mother and Father exchanged words, but they were too far away for me to hear. I don't think they were discussing my swimming style and spontaneity.

Grandmother Petronele was a mother of three daughters and six sons, Father being the oldest. Although she had been widowed a year before my parents were married in 1932, she managed to educate all her offspring through university and military academy while maintaining a four-building complex in Kaunas. This complex is still largely in family hands. The only exception is the lot facing the street. This became the property of some upper-level communist apparatchik.

It is interesting to note that many years later, during my office hours on Lovejoy in Buffalo, the receptionist announced that some Lithuanians from Kaunas were there to see me. They were ushered into one of the examining rooms. The man explained that they lived in front of my Grandmother on Kapsu Street. I had a polite but cold conversation with them and excused myself because of a full waiting room. They left and I dialed the local FBI number. The agent who answered was very interested in my story. He thanked me for the call and implied that the Bureau was aware of the "tourists" who had just made a courtesy call at my office.

In the late thirties, Grandmother Petronele became interested in acquiring property in the country. I had a real ball traveling with her and uncle Alfonsas in the rumble seat of his Chevrolet. We covered most estates on the market within fifty or sixty kilometers of Kaunas. Finally, she discovered Trepalava. This farm complex was just over the hill from Sirviai. She learned that the owner was an inveterate gambler with many outstanding debts. In the fashion of an underworld kingpin, Grandmother put out the word that she was buying Trepalava's squire's paper (I.O.U's). After an appropriate amount was purchased she went to the debtor and became the mistress of Trepalava.

Trepalava was an easy twenty-minute walk over the hill from Sirviai. I spent my days and nights at both places.

There was a small birch grove behind the barns. In late summer it was full of boletus mushrooms. There were absolutely no other varieties. Grandmother Petronele had them picked specifically to dry or marinate so they could be used in winter.

The only bad feature about Trepalava was the trail connecting the farm with the main road. It was OK in the summer when things were dry. In spring or late fall, however, it became one track of mud, impossible to drive on. One time Uncle Alfonsas decided that his Chevrolet could manage the muddy stretch. Well, he did manage it after a team of horses was hitched to the front bumper. Grandmother Petronele immediately ordered the car to be towed to the dry public road. She told my uncle, in no uncertain terms, to drive it back to Kaunas and not attempt such idiocy again.

In the early fall of 1939, Mother and I were walking in downtown Kaunas when we noticed a strangely painted military convoy. The trucks were full of soldiers in strange uniforms. People on the street recognized that this was the Polish army retreating after the fall of its country. Lithuania was neutral at that time, and the Poles were trying to escape German captivity by being interned at their neighbor's. This was the beginning of the end of my fun-filled, carefree childhood.

When the Russian occupation ended, our family moved to a splendid apartment in the medieval part of town, near the river Nemunas. Although my memory is not clear, I believe it was in late 1941 or early 1942.

One day Father took me on my first fishing trip, exposing me to the sport that would become one of my life's great enjoyments. He was supposed to teach me. Eventually, he did, but not before I became persistent in asking for the rod. He was having too good a time catching and releasing undersized fish about six inches in length. Father, as this vignette illustrates, was a devoted angler all his life.

Our apartment was only four buildings away from the river. Since it was so close, I was often able to dig up worms and go fishing. I had a lot of fun, but never caught anything longer than five or six inches. Well, that was a good start that led to my catching a 220 pound marlin off the shores of Cabo San Lucas many, many years later.

While living in the Old Town, Grandmother Olga became sick. She was hospitalized several times and had to undergo surgery. After her final hospitalization, she was brought to our apartment. Many years later Mother told me that Grandmother Olga died of carcinoma of the uterine cervix. During her last weeks she had widespread metastatic disease. She required frequent and ever-increasing doses of pain medications that were not available in the local pharmacies.

Fortunately, my Aunt Bernice (Brone) was working at the university hospital. At that time the hospital had been requisitioned exclusively for German military use. They too had difficulty obtaining opiates. She had access to Dolophine, better known today as methadone. Dolophine is a synthetic that had to fill in when morphine was not available. Aunt Bernice "requisitioned" the analgesic for my Grandmother Olga. How she got away with it in a German military hospital is a mystery to this day.

I was temporarily moved to Grandmother Petronele's in the New Town. After staying there for several weeks, I was taken back to our apartment. I was told absolutely nothing on the way. The walk from the Gamziukas homestead on Kapsu Street to our new home on Druskininku Street was quite long. During the war, however, there was no urban transportation available because the Germans had requisitioned all extant gasoline. Even walking was encumbered by a strictly enforced curfew. Darkness was complete after sunset. The blackout was total. There could be no street or window lights, and motor traffic was only visible by slits in the headlights.

On entering our home, I realized that something was very different. There was a scent of burning church candles! Through the partially open living-room door I saw two large candles impaled on candlestick holders standing on the floor. Between them was the head of a coffin. I opened the door. Inside the coffin was my Grandmother Olga. That was my first exposure to death within the family. I don't recall making an outburst, or even crying, at that time. I did cry later, however, when the coffin was closed and placed in a large sleigh. I recognized the horses from Sirviai. They took Grandmother Olga to the Boreisa family plot in Zeimiai cemetery. It was the winter of 1943.

Many years later, Helaine was told by Mother that Grandmother had known she was dying and asked to be laid out in a dress favored by Grandfather. There had been no undertakers available. They had all been pressed into service at the German military hospital to prepare German bodies for shipment to Germany. As a result, Mother had proceeded to dress her own dead mother in the requested dress. It was clear she had done a good job as no questions were put forward by those coming to pay their respects. Helaine asked her how it was possible to lay out her own mother in the coffin. She responded that when circumstances require extraordinary efforts, you do what you must do.

In the early nineties, Helaine and I visited the family grave at Zeimiai cemetery. It had been abandoned and was overgrown with weeds. Maybe Grandfather's sister Veronica cared for it until she died. More likely the last person to water the flowers was Mother, way back, forty-eight years ago.

In 1992 we walked on the road that was once the Main Street of Sirviai. The poplar tree and a wayside cross in a lilac bush were all that was left where Grandfather's farm buildings had been. The Russian front and the ensuing battle, moving through Sirviai in August of 1944, had burned everything down. I try to picture those old thatched roofs catching the first sparks. Were the animal-barn doors opened or did the fine horses perish in the inferno? Were the dogs, at least, turned loose? Or did they also become victims of the war? Indeed, those peaceful, happy days of my youth went up in smoke, seen only by the poplar and an old cross in the lilac bush. The lilac somehow protected the cross from both the Bolsheviks and the fury of the front.

The new Sirviai is totally without the charm I remember from 48 years ago. It consists of cookie-cutter, electrified, gas-heated, cinder block houses. What used to be a dusty, centuries old public road is now covered with asphalt.

At the turn of the road to the southeast, the old school house, which I had attended for half of a year, was still there. Abandoned and overgrown with weeds and bushes, it represents the early steps of my academic career.

We looked from the top of the hill in the direction of Trepalava. That land as I remember it is gone, long gone. It became a victim of communist "amelioration", the supposed improvement of land topography for easier access by farm machinery. After amelioration the land never again produced the bountiful harvest its owners had gathered, year after year, for many generations. The poor harvests of Trepalava and the surrounding countryside are testimonials to the agricultural failure of communism.

We did not see the inside of the church of Zeimiai because it was locked, but the outside of this gothic, brick building did not appear changed. I thought of the Sunday of my first Holy Communion which I had received here so many years ago. The right steeple had been tilted by a wind storm during the German occupation. It was perfectly perpendicular now.

The mausoleums in the church yard were filled with gardening implements. The coffins holding the remains of all local nobility had been buried in the town cemetery. Directly behind and to the west of the church stands a monument over the grave of the pastor of the late forties who was murdered by local communist toughs. To the right of the church yard gate stands a brand new Lithuanian wayside shrine. That marker is a great symbol of Lithuanian renaissance!

During the first Russian occupation, in 1940, most of the Lithuanian army was incorporated into the Soviet armed forces. High ranking officers, however, were discharged to the reserve. All of them were either executed in Lithuania or exiled to Siberia where they eventually died.

No one knows what happened to the fledgling Lithuanian aircraft industry. Planes previously ordered by the Air Force of Finland were never delivered. All Lithuanian-made airplanes disappeared into the vast spaces of the Motherland.

During the first hours of German attack, Uncle Victor, a junior officer in the Lithuanian army, simply took off, disappeared, deserted. So did over 90% of all enlisted men and officers that were not in Russian prisons.

Not all deserted, however! We knew one officer who retreated with the Red Army. Helen, Father's oldest sister, was this officer's wife. In the summer of 1944, he returned to Lithuania with the "liberating Red Army". Isn't this the quintessential oxymoron?

Their family had two more daughters. Uncle Frank was promoted to major general of the Soviet army and later, allegedly, became defense commissar of the Soviet Socialist Republic of Lithuania. He and his family were given a state apartment of sheer luxury, supposedly next door to the chief of the Lithuanian Committee for State Security; i.e., the Chief of the Lithuanian KGB. This was not a worrisome event. As we soon found out, connections have their advantages.

By now, in the second half of 1944, the family was scattered. My immediate family was in Wattens, near Innsbruck. Aunt Nina (Jane), her husband Albert Tarulis, and their newborn son Vytas were somewhere in Thuringia. Uncle Vladas got as far as Köenigsberg, East Prussia. He found out about the failed assassination of Hitler and boarded a freighter for Finland. There he dug antitank trenches and met up with some other Lithuanians, among them a fellow whose name was Baltakis. Uncle Vladas and Baltakis stole a boat and crossed the border river into neutral Sweden. This is where my uncle started the Swedish side of the Gamziukas family. Baltakis went to the United States. He became a Franciscan brother, and then a priest. Eventually, he was consecrated a bishop.

One wintry day of late 1945, Grandmother Petronele, Uncle John, and Uncle Valiukas (Valentine) were in Trepalava. "It was already dusk," Uncle Valiukas related to me, "There was a loud knock on the door." He thought it was the Lithuanian Brothers of the Forest, a partisan group. The fact was quite the opposite. It was the local NKVD (National Committee for Internal Affairs, an early name for the KGB). This group consisted of local nobodies who saw a personal opportunity in selling out to the Russians. They informed Uncle Valiukas that he was under arrest for anti-Soviet activities and accused him of supporting Lithuanian Partisans.

He was placed in a sleigh pulled by two horses. Under the command of a local female NKVD operative they proceeded to Zeimiai, the local township headquarters and police station. While the sleigh was pulled through a swale, the female told Valiukas, "If you are innocent I will release you now." My uncle saw this as an idiot's attempt to get praise for shooting an individual attempting to escape. He did not take the bait. That night he was locked up.

Grandmother Petronele set out for Vilnius the next day. She went to see Helen and found her son-in-law, now a major general, at home. She laid out the case and asked for help. In a few days Valiukas was set free.

Everything looked good. The family had strings to pull and pulled them wisely. Later, it became obvious that the situation had been more dangerous to Uncle Frank than Valiukas, the so-called enemy of the people. Valiukas would have been executed. But the major general would have been hung out to dry in some gulag for having Valiukas as a relative.

In 1992 Helaine and I visited the general and his new wife; Aunt Helen had died a few years before. The general and his new wife lived in a luxurious apartment. They treated us to tea and cakes. We exchanged a few polite absurdities and left after a brief visit. His wife, whose name escapes me, noted that my mother was a Boreisaite (maiden for Boreisa), and that she had been well known in the highest strata of pre-war society. My response to her was perhaps haughty but exceedingly polite.

There was a time during the German occupation (1941-1944) that the Gamziukas/Petronele household was on "autopilot". Grandmother lived in Trepalava while Uncle John, Uncle Vladas, and Aunt Genevieve were in Kaunas. Uncle Alfonsas, his wife Aldona (a fine lady who was German by birth), and their daughter Raminta lived in their own house on Zemaiciu Street. Uncle Victor and Aunt Bernice lived in an attic apartment on Kapsu Street.

Aunt Genevieve was attending the Kaunas Academy of Medicine. She developed tuberculosis with only a year to go before she would have become a physician. It appears no one noticed Genevieve's progressive cough and loss of weight until it was too late, even at the Academy where someone on the faculty should have recognized the warning signs.

Eventually, the diagnosis of advanced tuberculosis was made. She was taken to a sanatorium at St. Blasien in the Black Forest, in the deep southwest of Germany. The following summer, when I was 9, I corresponded with her very frequently. Summer came and went, but she remained febrile and surgery had to be delayed. The clinical picture remained bleak throughout the winter of 1943-1944, and the sanatorium finally informed the family that nothing more could be done for her.

In late winter, Father obtained a visa to go to Germany and bring her home, despite the fact that the country was now being bombed regularly and massively. He rented a private RR coach, and he and Aunt Helen prepared to go. The day before their departure, however, Father was called in by the Gestapo and informed that his visa had been revoked. When he inquired as to the reason, the Gestapo official simply stated, "Your wife is a Jewess." Someone not too well disposed to father had "blown him in"! It took several hours to correct the situation, but the required documents were provided. Mother, after all, was an "Aryan"; using Nazi definition of the word.

The sad journey commenced. My favored Aunt Genia was brought home. We took care of her until she died during the Holy Week of 1944. She was buried on Easter Sunday.

We spent Christmas of 1943, our last in Lithuania, in Sirviai. Four kids, including me, went into Grandfather's forest to cut down a Christmas tree. We thought we were really brave. In winter the wolves were considered dangerous, but we didn't pay attention to the warnings. I guess doing that was sort of a rite of passage. Imagine a group of kids, with no adults present, surrounded by a wintry forest full of wolves licking their chops and circling dangerously around! We conquered our imagination, selected a nice fir, chopped it down, and brought it home.

The following spring was full of tension. The front was approaching. The possibility of a second Russian occupation, with all the horrors that would entail, loomed in the near future. We left Sirviai and returned to Kaunas. We did not stay there very long before returning to Sirviai again. I never learned why we made this short visit to the city.

This was our last short visit to Kaunas. Things were most unusual. None of our farm horses were there. Both father's and grandfather's cars had been confiscated in the fall of 1940 by local communists "for the benefit of the people." The horses that had brought us to Kaunas went right back to the country because they were needed for farm work.

For the first time, Mother, her friend Vera Petrovna, and I hitchhiked on Savanoriu Prospektas, the highway going northeast from Kaunas towards the Latvian city of Daugavpils. Vera Petrovna was very attached to me. She was not a relative, but a close friend of the family. Actually, I never knew her last name. Petrovna is patronymic for "daughter of Peter." I only knew that she was the sister of the wife of a good friend of Grandfather.

In those fear-laden, late-spring days, the highway was full of German military traffic going both ways. Occasionally, we would see civilian "gas generator" trucks. Gas generators were widely used throughout Europe. They had a contraption that looked like an oversize hot water tank. This was the generator. Wood was the fuel. Combustion, however, was purposely incomplete. The resultant gases were used to fuel the internal combustion engine. Such fuels were not exactly energy rich, and the vehicle moved at snail's pace. On encountering a steep hill, some of these vehicles had to be pushed by the passengers. Toward mid-afternoon we managed to hitch a ride in the back of one of these trucks.

The truck dropped us off at Jonava and continued on in a cloud of dust. It must have been six p.m. Ahead of us was a nine kilometer hike to Sirviai.

After walking to a hill called Bociu Kalnas, Mother decided to rest. *Loosely translated, Bociu Kalnas means "Hill of Ancient Warriors". Exactly 48 years later, while visiting Lithuania, we had a picnic at precisely the same spot.*

After a brief rest, Mother decided to continue. The next village was Vaivadiskiai. *It is still there today, totally untouched by the passage of the front that burned Sirviai to the ground.* We found relatively few people in the village. Most of them were working in the fields.

After a turn to the north, the road climbed a small knoll. At the top was an old cemetery used by both Vaivadiskiai and Sirviai. Sirviai was about one Km away and clearly visible. The sun touched the trees of Grandfather's woods to the west. The village, set against a dark northeastern backdrop, looked like a painting of the Flemish school. The evening was beautiful and peaceful with an approaching golden sunset. The familiar aroma of the countryside permeated the air.

We finally arrived in Sirviai. It was nice to enter the familiar surroundings, sit at the farm kitchen table, and have supper with the farm hands. The quiet end of this unusual day was the very beginning of my disarrayed and tumultuous life.

I cannot recall, through the mist of so many years, how long we stayed at the estate this last time. However, I do recall going through my possessions. Among much junk there was a Stone Age ax. It must have been from the late Stone Age because it was smooth. A hole in the handle was also smooth. Part of the ax had cracked off, probably many centuries ago. Recently, I concluded that my ax must still be there somewhere under the soil. The Russian front torched the village, but stones don't burn, do they?

That was my last visit to the countryside I loved so much.

How we found ourselves again in Kaunas, I just don't recall. It must have been by horse. This time we arrived at Grandmother Petronele's home on Kapsu Street. Father was already there. He related a story of leaving Vilnius with the cigarette company employee convoy, which had German military permits to move to Kaunas. The Russians were now on Lithuanian territory, very near Vilnius. His ride that night of some 100 Km was certainly not boring. The highway along their route was repeatedly attacked by Russian Shtormoviks targeting the retreating German army vehicles. Many times during the night he was forced to jump into adjacent ditches. A few times he plowed face first into a bunch of nettles which left terrible hives on his skin. It was fortunate for

Father that Russian aviation prowess was not as good as it became during the Korean and Vietnam wars.

The following day, Mother began to pack a minimum of necessities into an Opel Kapitan we would be sharing with professor Viliamas and his eighteen year old bride. That night, the car was taken to the Alcohol Trust Co. while we slept at Kapsu Street. To me, all of this looked like the beginning of a magnificent adventure. The next day we would be off to Germany!

The sun rose early for another gorgeous day. The sky was entirely cloudless and blue. This deep, clear blue is mentioned in many Lithuanian songs that go back to antiquity.

About six o'clock that evening, a truck picked us up and took us to the Alcohol Trust. I remember the scene vividly. Kapsu Street was paved with cobblestones, and it hadn't rained for many days. Dust rose behind the departing truck. The last image I remember is Vera Petrovna running behind the truck and waving. She then covered her face with both hands and disappeared in the dust. I have no idea what happened to her. The only person from that evening I ever saw again was Uncle Valiukas. The others were long dead when I returned in 1992, forty-eight years later.

Chapter Three

The convoy of Tobacco and Alcohol Trust cars pulled out of the trust building garage, made a left, and proceeded across Laisves Aleja. It drove through the medieval Kaunas, across the only bridge left that crossed the river Nemunas, and south on the highway leading towards Königsberg (now Kaliningrad).

As we crossed Laisves Aleja, I thought of the many times I had walked with Mother under the lindens of the median. I loved the knockwurst she bought for me from the street vendors. These vendors carried a veritable kitchen in the form of a stainless steel compartmentalized box. The sausages were cooked in a compartment that held boiling water. From another, the vendor would produce a roll and apply mustard. The knockwurst was then placed in a little paper boat and handed to me.

As our Opel sped south, dusk descended on the countryside. Fields were covered with patches of early summer mist. The air was saturated with the fragrance of new mown hay. Just like in Sirviai! Sirviai, which would probably never be seen again!

When our car reached the small town of Garliava, Father was directed by a soldier of the Feldgendarmerie, the German military police, to a side dirt road that led to a group of farm buildings. This was to be our encampment for the night. Our supper was food we had brought with us from Kapsu Street. After dinner we slept in a huge barn on beds made of stacked hay.

The next morning our breakfast was varied and unusual, at least to me. It consisted of bread, milk purchased from the farmer, some sausage, and a piece of unsliced, smoked bacon. There was no trichinosis in Lithuania; therefore, uncooked bacon was safe to eat.

I got to know some other kids of various executives of the Alcohol and Tobacco trusts. One of them could not eat strawberries. That was a new one to me! We found some wild strawberries in a little grove and ate them to our heart's content. They are always more flavorful and much tastier than the home grown variety. The kid who couldn't eat strawberries just watched us.

The convoy spent a whole week at this farm. I had no idea why. Much, much later Father explained that the Germans had stopped all withdrawal activities because their front held against the Russians on the other side of Vilnius. As a result, the convoy was ordered to return to Kaunas.

The city hadn't changed in our brief absence. Life seemed to be moving along normally. Strawberry vendors were more plentiful. It was high season for this popular berry. The main arterials were, of course, filled with military traffic. Traffic was directed by German Kopfjaeger: "head hunters". This was their own term for the MPs. Apparently, ordinary city police were employed elsewhere.

Kapsu Street was empty. Not even a pedestrian could be seen. Grandmother's home had been locked up and showed no sign of life. Using a public phone, Father found out that no one was answering in Karaliuna's apartment. Visinskio Street was also empty and the houses locked up. It was obvious to us where our relatives had all gone. The Karaliunas went to Sirviai. Grandmother, Aunt Helen, Uncle Vladas, and Uncle Jonas went to Trepalava. Current wisdom held it that it was safer in the country than in the city while the front rolled by. The fear of bombing raids was all pervasive. History, however, showed that Sirviai burned down while Kaunas was untouched.

Our family, including Grandfather Julian, moved into the vacant apartment of a wealthy businessman whom Father knew and who had already left for "The West".

During our first night in this lavish apartment, I realized the front was not that far away. My bed was a sofa in the study. Huge windows faced southeast and afforded a splendid view of downtown Kaunas and the river Nemunas beyond. The opulence of this view alone is enough to describe the upscale nature of the dwelling. To the east, in the direction of Vilnius, the sky was red from the light of burning towns. For a ten year old that was an awesome and frightening sight. The fires were not that far away, and the night was strangely silent. I could tell there was no activity at the front as we were so close the artillery would have easily been heard.

The following day, Mother and I set off to see if anyone was still at uncle Alfonsas's home. His house was located at the top of the eastern bank of the river Neris. The view from there was magnificent. It overlooked the suburb on the other side of the river, which in peacetime had a large Jewish population. During the early part of the German occupation, the Gestapo had ordered all Jews to move there, into what became a modern-day ghetto

While we were walking along the street, the sky suddenly thundered with explosions. Mother grabbed me and pulled me into the doorway of a small apartment house. I had no idea what was going on. There were the sounds of airplanes, and more explosions that left black smudges in the blue, almost cloudless sky. Exploding flak shells showered the city with shrapnel. These pieces could be as fatal as a bullet fired from a rifle.

After a few minutes the commotion stopped. Mother explained that the Germans had been shooting at Russian planes. Well, that was my second exposure to actual acts of war within three years. I was very interested and by no means scared.

We found Uncle Alfonsas and Aunt Aldona packing. They were joining us in our little convoy about to set out for Germany. Cousin Raminta, who now holds a PhD in German studies, was just a toddler, befuddled by all that was going on around her. Uncle Alfonsas had a car, but I cannot recall the make. It was no longer the Chevrolet with the rumble seat.

Father arranged for him to get official travel orders which would allow him to refuel at military supply points. I don't know who Father bribed, nor how much he had to pay. In retrospect, many years later, I realized that he must have had to be careful. Trying to bribe a hard-core Nazi could be dangerous. But one of Father's characteristics was highly developed street smarts!

Uncle's small, immaculately kept home always fascinated me for what it contained. Several paintings by known Lithuanian artists, a spinet piano and, most intriguing of all, a piece of amber the size of a fist. Uncle Alfonsas had found it many years before while walking on the beach in Palanga.

Years later, I drew, from memory, a picture of the splendid amber find. After entering Uncle's house in 1992, Helaine recognized the piece from my drawing. It was sitting, as it had for all those years, in the sunlight on a little table next to the piano.

After a brief visit, Mother and I returned to the apartment to make final preparations for the next day's journey. The Russians had resumed the offensive, and the German military government had lifted the ban on travel to the West. I got the impression that the order was saying, in effect, to get out while the getting was good.

Our last day in Kaunas dawned early, and the weather was very promising. The funicular to downtown was not running anymore, so we walked to the Alcohol Trust. Our group boarded the same vehicles we had been in before and once again left downtown Kaunas. This time we headed west.

Our convoy crossed the Neris bridge. As it was about to enter the Zemaiciu Highway, the car in front of us slowed down and stopped. We all stopped and got out. To the east, less than one kilometer away, the ghetto was burning! Flames reached high into the morning sky. This conflagration was not an accident. Much later, in Augsburg, it became common knowledge that the fire had been deliberately set by the SS.

There, behind the rising smoke, high on the east bank of Neris, were Kapsu and Giedraiciu streets, and the memories of a happy childhood.

The convoy continued. Every so many kilometers we encountered German Feldgendarmerie (M.P.) checkpoints. These military police had Schmeisser machine pistols positioned across their chests. Around their necks hung crescent-shaped metal plates stamped with an eagle and swastika. The M.P.'s were checking ID papers and, most importantly, documents justifying travel on this road, at this time, and in this direction. Father had all the required papers. Also, our windshield displayed the name of our organization and destination. These papers were marked with a multitude of eagle and swastika seals. Germans sure liked to slap seals on any document.

Toward evening, we pulled into the yard of a prosperous looking manor. I recall being very hungry. As kids do, I started voicing this fact aloud. It was clearly understood by everyone that what we were going to eat was what we had brought with us. There would be no feeding stations or ration distribution points. So this first day on the road we had a supper not unlike the breakfast of less than two weeks ago. After supper we bedded down in the barn.

In the morning, we kids discovered that the manor had a large pond. Questions arose. Were there fish there? And if so, where would we get the tackle to catch them? Well, we soon learned from a nearby farm hand that there were, indeed, fish in that pond. Our second question was answered shortly thereafter. One of Father's friends was an avid fisherman who had not left his fishing equipment behind for the Russians. He outfitted all of us kids with a hook, bobber, and line. Finding a rod was our problem. This was quickly solved when someone observed that there were hazelnut bushes nearby. In a pinch, hazelnut wood makes a workable fishing rod. Worms, of course, were no problem. Soon we were catching a type of fish called karosas. Some sort of crappie, I guess. We had many hours of fantastic fishing. Since no one wanted to cook them, we threw them back. The fun in fishing is catching, not eating.

The convoy people purchased a pig from the manor owner, had it slaughtered, and spent the rest of a week eating it. Why a week? It seems that to proceed further the convoy had to obtain yet another permit.

Since our cars were loaded with good quality cigarettes, there was no problem with greasing German palms. Once permission from the Feldgendarmerie was obtained, the cars got going again in the direction of Skaudvile and East Prussia.

About mid-afternoon of the next day, Uncle Alfonsas pulled over to the side of the road, got out of his car, and walked over to ours. Father inquired if there was a problem with the vehicle and got a negative answer. The problem was infinitely more profound. Uncle Alfonsas had been giving the entire enterprise of leaving Lithuania much thought during the previous week. He had just come to his decision now, here on the highway. He announced that he would not proceed any further. Instead, he would return to the manor and then home. This was quite a surprise for all of us. A bad argument flared up between the two oldest brothers of the Gamziukas family. Each tried to convince the other that the course on which he was about to embark was not wise. The exchange lasted for some time. Eventually, the brothers separated in anger, never to see each other again.

Mother and Aunt Aldona were crying as they tried to avert this family disaster. However, their efforts were to no avail. Uncle Alfonsas simply felt that he could not leave his country. The convoy continued west while Uncle Alfonsas made a U-turn and returned east.

Towards evening, the truck driven by Grandfather was directed by military police to pull into the long driveway of another prosperous manor. This driveway was lined with beautiful, old linden trees which in the waning daylight looked like some majestic canopy. Again we stopped in the area of the barn where we spent the first of five nights sleeping in the hay loft.

It was now late July. The weather remained sunny and warm. We bought fresh food from the locals and kept the staples in the car untouched.

The morning after the convoy arrived, we kids discovered a gully with a small stream behind the manor complex. To our great joy we soon discovered that the stream contained fish! Out came our tackle, rods were again made out of hazelnut sticks, worms were dug up, and we were in business. This time one of the other kids managed to hook into a northern pike. Alas, he had equipment failure. The rod broke and then the line. The pike got away. This stoked our enthusiasm to no end. Each of us thought *maybe the next pike will be on my hook!* It never happened.

On the afternoon of the sixth day, the convoy left the manor and proceeded towards the German border.

It was completely dark when I woke up to someone shouting in German. It was an SS officer yelling at Father. To my surprise, Father was yelling back at him, also in German and with equal vigor. I knew German rank insignias for both the Wehrmacht and theWaffen-SS. This German was only a Sturmfuehrer, the equivalent of a second lieutenant in our army. A mere JOP, junior officer present, in the parlance of an American armed forces officers club. And yet, the guy was threatening Father with a machine pistol! Abruptly, however, he shut up and waved us through. I had no idea what had happened, or why the junior Hitler suddenly shut up and let us pass.

Many years later Father told me the story. He had accidentally switched on the headlights while the convoy was in total darkness and Russian planes were roaming about. The German had flipped out and threatened to execute him. Father explained to me that Germans of that ilk are best handled by taking an authoritative posture. Father had begun saying, actually shouting, that such traffic management inefficiency in the sixth year of the war was criminal. He had demanded to know who and where was this junior Hitler's commanding officer. At this point the Sturmfuehrer had backed off.

I never had before seen such traffic. Convoys such as ours were minute. The road was full of vehicles. Ambulances and trucks filled with German wounded were traveling west. Some trucks were filled with disheveled troops trying to sleep. Some of these soldiers appeared to have bandages on them. Several kuebel wagens carrying officers passed the decrepit military column. The remains of the proud Wehrmacht, victorious though they had been in Sirviai, were a pathetic lot. Tractors pulled platforms loaded with either supplies, or antiaircraft guns and their crews. Ambulances were full and did not stop at the many hospitals that had been requisitioned for the Army. The hospitals themselves were evacuating. Traffic going east carried fresh looking soldiers. These vehicles, however, were comparatively few in number. Occasionally, tanks went by, in pairs or threes, raising unbelievable clouds of dust.

Much later in my life, I served as a surgeon in an American armored battalion. I acquired enough basic knowledge of armored movement to realize that on that particular day the German Mark IV tanks had not been led or coordinated in any tactical fashion. They were the highest priority vehicles, and their drivers simply did not give a damn if they pushed civilian vehicles off the road.

It was just past 11:20 p.m. on the automobile clock when I noticed a Lithuanian road sign that read "German border 100 meters." Sure enough, there in the dark, merged together, were the Lithuanian and German frontier stations. That evening, in the midst of chaotic military traffic, I left the country of my birth. I would not return for 48 years. When I did return for a visit, I was an American.

Chapter Four

Morning dawned and was rather misty. The kind of mist that burns off as the sun rises. Just ahead was another military check point. It was acting as a combination immigration and military control post. While our papers were being checked, a Wehrmacht captain came to the driver's window. He asked Father if there was room in the car to take a wounded soldier to an aid station some five kilometers down the road. The poor soldier was "walking wounded". Russian saboteurs had been dropped by parachute to cause disruption behind the lines. They had shot him through upper right arm. The wound had been dressed and his arm placed in a makeshift sling. That was, and still is, the medical care that one gets at a dressing station in a time of war. A superficial, stop gap measure.

He must have been given pain medication because he was slightly obtunded and quietly kept asking for "Mutti" (mommy). The poor soldier could not have been older than seventeen or eighteen. This was as close as the war got to me. I was going on 11 years of age and felt very, very sorry for this kid.

The convoy entered Tilsit (now Sovetsk). The city looked very nice. There were absolutely no signs of war. No bomb craters, ruins, or burned out buildings. Soon, our car approached the bridge crossing the Nemunas. Here, however, they called the river Memel. It was much wider than in Kaunas as the estuary was much nearer.

With the city behind us, our progress continued in a colossal concentration of military traffic going in both directions. The Feldgendarmerie were going nuts at major intersections, but only occasionally stopped a westbound military vehicle. They all had a Marschbefehl (marching order) pasted to their windshields.

The highway on which we were traveling was macadamized. I never saw any such roads back home. There only city streets had asphalt on them. The medieval parts of Kaunas were paved with cobblestone.

Eventually, our convoy turned off the main road to Insterburg and entered the square yard of a prosperous looking farm. We kids observed that a fat German sergeant, who had accompanied us from the very start and spoke fluent Lithuanian, abruptly quit using Lithuanian and switched entirely to the language of the "Vaterland" (fatherland). The bastard wouldn't answer anyone, even us kids, except in German! I often wonder what happened to the overfed Teuton. Did he get killed? Did he survive the war? Did he wind up in Siberia as a POW? Or is he living somewhere down the street in Buffalo? He was not a Nazi, but definitely a survivor who knew his business.

After a short stay at this farm, we were parceled out, family by family, to neighboring farms. Our cars were confiscated by the military. We felt to be in limbo. Late that afternoon, our family arrived at another, smaller, East Prussian farm. This would be our temporary home. One had to be blind not to see the order and beauty of both the fields and the buildings. After all, East Prussia was Germany's bread basket. For dinner that day some farm woman brought us bread, something tomato-colored, ersatz coffee, and a saucer containing something that looked like sugar. Mother stirred some of this crystalline substance into her cup and promptly announced that it was salt! The menu, as you can see, was limited.

The next morning I met some of the German kids. They were very friendly to me even though, unlike both my parents, I didn't know a word of German.

The farm had a big pond where I saw a large pike just under the surface! My "fishing rod", however, was now in the hands of the Wehrmacht, along with our car. So much for that enterprise.

Grandfather spent time with me since he had nothing to do and I was full of questions. I had already read all of the home newspapers we had used for wrapping various items. We had not brought any Lithuanian books. I was developing home-sickness already. "When are we going back to Kaunas and Sirviai?" I asked him. There was a great foreboding in him when he answered, "Probably never." Indeed, for him the words told the absolute truth as we will see later. As for me, I had had enough of this great adventure of going to Germany. Home, home is where I wanted to go.

A few days later, after helping the farmer with some work, Father went back to the place where the other members of the convoy were meeting that evening. Before he returned, Russian planes started bombing Insterburg. It was shortly after dark, and the flak was infinitely more intense than in Kaunas. The flak bursts were rather low this time, indicating a low altitude attack. Because it was dark, we could see the actual explosion of the flak shells. At times the sound, terrible and overwhelming, was continuous. It came from the direction of where Father had gone while it was still light. By now I understood what flak shrapnel could do, and I knew that Father had to walk along an open road for several kilometers with flak bursts over his head.

Meanwhile, the rest of the family huddled together with the farm people inside the stone basement. After some thirty or forty minutes of looking anxiously out of the cellar window, I recognized Father by the light of the flak burst. He was walking quickly, not running, through the gate. After the raid was over, he told Mother and Grandfather that the day after next we would be taking an express to Vienna.

The Insterburg railway station was similar to that of Kaunas, but it was much smaller. After a considerable wait, the Königsberg – Vienna express arrived late in the afternoon. We had to go through another police check. This time they checked our ID's, papers allowing entry into Germany, and papers justifying the trip. If we were missing even one of these documents the policemen would call the Gestapo, who were always present in the railway stations. It was anybody's guess what would happen to us in the hands of the Gestapo.

The date was the sixth of August, 1944. One might ask how this date could be remembered after all these years. The answer is simple. I still have the original ticket under the glass cover of a table in my library. The rail tickets in Lithuania and Germany were small pieces of hard cardboard. That was very practical. They could be carried in any pocket without being damaged.

We passed the security check and boarded the train. There were many available seats in the second class compartments, but few were together. Mother and I found two adjoining seats in one compartment, while Father and Grandfather wound up in the next carriage.

The train pulled out very promptly and soon I was looking at the passing panorama of East Prussia. Well-kept farms and paved roads flew past the window. I saw no forests. The land was monotonously flat. I felt like we were traveling on the surface of a gigantic pancake.

It was already after dark when we made our first stop in Allenstein. The station was fully lit and extremely busy. The platform was loaded with civilians carrying many suitcases and bundles. They were most likely refugees, just like us. Standing among them were soldiers with rifles and rucksacks. The ubiquitous MP's were randomly checking the papers of individual soldiers. These checks were anything but perfunctory. Every check started with an examination of the soldier's pay book. Each solider had to show a typewritten document that most likely explained why he was not at the front.

Much later I discovered that these random checks were conducted to discourage desertions. It was a mystery to me how this was much of a deterrent. What prevented a deserter from boarding a local train at a small station? Small stations had neither police nor Gestapo. Neither did local trains. Theoretically, a person could cross Germany by boarding a local train and changing to another each time one reached its final destination. It wouldn't be healthy to get caught, however, and all deserters were dealt with the same way. They were shot. In those days the Germans were great when it came to final solutions.

The train was still in the station when suddenly all the lights went out. Everything was cast into total darkness. It was an air raid! Later on, I discovered that precautionary measures were taken before known enemy formations could target one's location. Accordingly, we heard no sirens, explosions, or aircraft.

The train started moving. It accelerated as if in a hurry to get out of the station. An army captain, who shared our compartment, explained to Mother that enemy planes were somewhere inside the front lines and that the blackout was routine. The curtains in our compartment were drawn shut. There were two blue lights at the ceiling, so we still could make each other out after our eyes got accustomed to the depressing twilight.

European trains in those days had carriage-connecting passages called harmonicas. This train was not so full that people had to sit on suitcases in the corridors or harmonicas.

We continued through the night toward Torn. At that point I knew the train was in Poland. When it became light, however, I noticed the differences. The landscape before me looked rather beat up and primitive. Muddy dirt roads were at the grade crossings. Houses along the track looked old and not well maintained, if they were maintained at all. What a difference from Lithuania or East Prussia!

The journey was rather monotonous until Torn and Posen (Poznan) were well behind us and we entered Germany proper. The landscape changed to rolling hills and then to low mountains. This was my first exposure to mountains. One has to remember that the highest point in Lithuania is only 339 meters above sea level.

Soon after we entered the Reich, two clean-cut, polite gentlemen entered the compartment. They flashed their Gestapo warrant badges and asked for ID papers. They first asked Mother, who showed them her Lithuanian passport. One of them examined it closely, almost giving the impression that Lithuanian was within his linguistic repertoire. He then inquired, again very politely, about her permission to enter and travel in Germany. Mother explained that her husband was in the first compartment of the next carriage and had their papers. The German asked his assistant to see Father. He then proceeded to engage in an inconsequential conversation with my Mother, who was now very nervous. Soon the junior agent confirmed her story. The two of them apologized for that formality and left the compartment. I spoke no German, but had the feeling that what had just happened had been very threatening. However, the journey continued with no further disturbances.

Toward late afternoon we crossed the Danube. What a sight it was! I had never dreamed that rivers could be so wide. The length of the bridge seemed never ending.

In a few more minutes the train rolled into the Nordbahnhof (north station) and came to a stop. All the station signs carried the name Wien. What was Wien? "Vienna," explained Grandfather. We had traveled 1060 km from Insterburg.

No one bothered us with ID checks as we left the station. Outside was a wonderful world, different from any I had ever known. A world class city!

Street cars! I had seen them only in pictures or movies. People were everywhere. Many were in uniform, especially in and around the station.

What was left of our "convoy" gathered outside the station and had a brief conference about how to proceed from there. The decision was made to take a street car as cabs were not available and the address we had been given was too far for a walk.

The street car traveled part of the way along the Ring Strasse. I was awed by the magnificent buildings, broad avenues, and crowds on the sidewalks. There were no bombed out structures, no signs of war. It was late summer in 1944, and Vienna had not been bombed even once.

Finally, the street car stopped. We carried our possessions as we walked to a large building on, and I never forgot this name, Gaensebachergasse (Goose Stream Street). When we arrived, a huge negro was standing in front of the main door. I had never seen a black man before. We kids were brought up not to stare at anything so we didn't, but the temptation was great.

We entered the building, and the first thing we noticed were many huge hall-like rooms with high ceilings. They were filled with made-up beds. I don't recall if they were "co-ed" or not. Supper was served in one of the rooms that had been converted into a "Speiseraum" (a dining hall). Afterwards we settled down for the night.

This building was symbolic of German "Ordnung" (order). They were prepared to handle large numbers of transient refugees. The only problem with the "Ordnung" was that there were bedbugs in those beds. I had never seen bedbugs before, just like I had never seen street cars.

We did not stay long in Vienna. During those few days, Grandfather and I took some walks together. Since our dormitory was a long way from the Ring, there was nothing interesting to see. Grandfather did not speak the local lingo too well, so we did not take the street car out of the immediate area. Eventually, our convoy traveled on.

One morning we found ourselves at the Suedbahnhof (south station) waiting for a local train to take us to Neudoerfl, a village located just south of Wiener Neustadt, the great Messerschmitt works center. There were no uniforms or Gestapo at this station. Nobody but an old conductor checking tickets. He looked as if he must have been checking tickets at the time of Franz Joseph.

The seats on the local train were all wooden, and it stopped at every town. This type of train was called "Personenzug" and traveled no more than 100 km. Express trains were out of the question if you had to travel long distances and did not have work and travel justification papers. As mentioned before, they always had Gestapo on board. The local, on the other hand, almost never did. Therefore, it was possible to travel the length and width of The Reich by taking successive local trains.

In Neudoerfl we left our luggage at the little station and walked to our new "home". A series of one-story wooden barracks stood along the side of a highway, next to a large forest. The highway led to the border of Hungary. Across the road, in the distance, stood a huge complex of Messerschmitt factories.

Each of the barracks had rooms with multiple two-tiered beds, and several families were assigned to each room. After getting their room assignments, the men of the convoy returned to the station to retrieve the luggage. The Station master, another Franz Joseph relic, must have been favorably impressed by my family's outward appearance because he offered us the only luggage cart to use to transport our suitcases, provided that we return it before dark! The total distance must have been no more than two kilometers.

The compound had a kitchen barrack and a laundry/bath building. All the comforts of home, albeit a one-room home that had to be shared with strangers. Well, we Lithuanians managed not to have any other nationalities in our rooms. Belgians and French shared the camp with us. They had been brought to Germany to work in war production. They had their own barracks and were just as happy to not share a space with us as we were delighted to not mix with them.

Life became fun again for us kids. We wandered into the woods and found strange things. For example, we found some seats halfway up a tree, reachable by a makeshift ladder. Some of the men had hunted back home and explained to us that these were hunting stands or seats. Then one of the kids found a snake with yellow cheeks. Was it poisonous? Again, adult outdoorsmen among us taught us that these were harmless adders. Another animal we found that we had never seen back home was a tiny tree frog . The only thing these forests did not have was mushrooms.

The woods stretched to the southwest where a huge mountain loomed on the horizon. Though it could not be high in an international catalogue of mountains, and was totally covered by deciduous trees, to us it might as well have been Mount Everest. There simply are no mountains in all of Lithuania.

One day, while wandering through those woods, we emerged on the other side. A wide valley opened up before us. Both slopes were covered with vineyards. We had all tasted grapes in Lithuania, but we also knew them to be imported. Grapes do not grow that far north in Europe. There was no one in sight so we helped ourselves to the grapes. They were tasty but nothing exceptional. Personally, I thought that Grandfather's apples in Sirviai, from one tree in particular, were the fruit to beat. Even now, after traveling around the globe and visiting 78 countries, I have never found a fruit that could beat those Renata apples I ate while sitting on my favorite branch in Sirviai.

The first really sunny day the air raid sirens sounded at about nine am. There was little undulation in their frightening screams. After three minutes all was quiet. "What was the meaning of this?" all the new arrivals asked. Soon, everyone knew. This was "Voralarm", and it meant enemy bombing formations had entered German airspace. "Enemy" was not really our enemy. It was the American air force. However, as we were within sight of a German aircraft production facility the chance of trouble coming our way was fairly high.

Sure enough, about one hour later, the sirens wailed again. But this time the undulations were much closer together, sending a message of urgency. This pattern of siren scream meant enemy formations were flying in the direction of our city. Soon we could see fighters attacking the heads of contrails. A silver point at the head of the contrail signified an American bomber. From a distance the sky was a beautiful, fascinating show. We were totally unafraid. We somehow thought that things were happening too far away to hurt us. We were that stupid! There were no air raid shelters, but our parents chased us inside the barracks. That's when flak opened up. The air filled with these bursts, and shrapnel fell to the ground.

In about thirty minutes, the whole show was over. We kids ran outside and started collecting the metal pieces on the ground! After a few weeks, it became obvious that the raids were a common occurrence. Shrapnel was not an unusual find. Nobody was hurt by any of these raids, but the shrapnel showers made everyone take cover.

One day, some members of the convoy went to Vienna to attend a meeting organized by Viennese Lithuanians. I don't know that anything practical resulted. I guess meeting other Lithuanians and spending some time with them was the ultimate reward. Word came back, however, that we had better get jobs away from the Red Juggernaut's advance or the Arbeitsamt (labor office) would send us to work in Graz. That was Austria's second largest city, and it was in the direct path of Russian armies. Thus began the scramble for work as far west as possible.

A week or so later, on a nice Sunday, some of the convoy people went back to Vienna for sightseeing. Our family was among them. On leaving the

Suedbahnhof we took a street car to the Hotel Regina. This hotel was situated very close to the Votivskirche, a beautiful gothic church constructed in the late 19th century. Years later, I discovered that a Lutheran church on Genesee Street in Buffalo, also of gothic architecture, had been built in 1848. Not all churches in Vienna are that old after all.

After we had lunch at the hotel, the group toured Vienna. We saw Schoenbrun Palace, the Gloriette, and the adjoining zoo. Then we traveled to St. Stephen's Cathedral and, eventually, Prater. To a Lithuanian kid in 1944, Prater was the equivalent of Disney World to an American kid in the late twentieth century. The giant Ferris wheel, called Riesenrad, was really something. The people-carrying compartments were the size of small streetcars!

During the course of the day, we saw no evidence of air-raid damage to this wonderful city. Most large cities were being bombed into rubble, but Vienna was untouched. This was soon to change, but by then we were out of the area.

That night's dinner was my very first exposure to dining out. I was very impressed with the surroundings and waiters. I cannot remember being impressed with food. Well, there was a war on.

I next saw "Wien" in 1969, twenty-five years after the capitulation. Neither Helaine nor I saw any remnants of the destruction brought about by the street fighting in 1945. The only place that had a scar was the area near the Gloriette. I think the scar was left there as a memorial. Our guide, with considerable bitterness, ascribed the damage to indiscriminate American bombing. If he had added that Austria had been an occupied victim of Nazi Germany, I would have choked right up.

About a month later, Father announced that he had gotten a job at a cigarette paper factory in Tyrol, a town near Innsbruck. Tyrol? I had never heard of it. Well, as time went by arrangements were made to travel. It seems that the cigarette company father managed back in Vilnius used to buy the paper from the company in Wattens. Wattens, by the way, is the world headquarters of the Swarovsky Corporation, the world renown manufacturer of fine optics and crystal.

Sometime in early October, we said good-bye to the remaining members of our convoy and boarded the local to Vienna. At the Westbahnhof, we transferred to the Munich Express and continued our odyssey. The train was packed. Grandfather and Mother found a seat in a compartment, but Father and I had to sit on our suitcases. And not just in the corridor, but in the harmonica! After a most uncomfortable night, the express reached Rosenheim. Surprisingly, we never encountered any Gestapo on that train.

We got out and boarded a local going south. Soon, the station sign "Woergl" appeared. This was our new interim destination. Our original convoy was many miles back. I wondered if I would ever see any of them again.

We had lunch at a small Gasthaus across the square from the terminal. Here the waitress asked for ration cards. Just before we had left Neudoerfl, the administration had issued travel ration cards. Without these cards one could get only un-rationed food. As far as I know, that meant only seasonal vegetables.

After lunch, we proceeded down a street that crossed under the railway tracks and led toward the river Inn. A fenced in barrack area stood on the shore of the river. The buildings looked well maintained and had nicely paved driveways and sidewalks. The gate had gothic sign that read "Durchgangs Lager, Woergl" (Transit Camp, Woergl).

A small room was assigned to us. Then we had to have a shower and medical exam. That was a totally new experience for me. After the ablution in a barrack-type shower shared with some other men who spoke an unfamiliar language, we were ushered into an adjoining room for the physical. We were all standing there stark-naked when a pretty German nurse walked in. After a brief conversation with those who spoke German, she performed the physicals. Complete!

After leaving this health facility, we found out that Mother and the other women were subjected to the same procedure with one difference. While they were standing around naked in the room, a *male* nurse walked in and did a cursory exam. Fortunately, that was the only indignity we experienced.

After a few more days of document verification, we left for Wattens. On the way to the station, we were passed a guarded column of Italian men and women headed in the opposite direction. I had no idea what that was all about. Later, Father told me they had been brought to work in the German war industry. When I asked him why they had been accompanied by armed guard, Father said he did not know.

The weather was sunny. I admired the foothills of the Alps, and also looked with amazement at the rail technology. The trains here ran on electricity! There were wires above the tracks, and boxy-looking locomotives had bars on their roofs that touched the overhead wires for energy. There was no smoke, no bad odor, and no dirt. Very neat.

During the train ride the sky became cloudy, and a slight drizzle began to fall. After a short ride we saw the station sign for Fritzens-Wattens.

This station, situated on the left bank of the Inn, was actually in Fritzens. Wattens was on the other side and considerably larger. The town was typically Tyrolean. Ordinary buildings were scattered among the more numerous Chalets, some of which had beautiful frescoes on their front walls. The south end of town seemed to climb the southern range of the Inn valley. The famous Swarovski crystal works were located on the east side of a ravine that descended from the mountains. The crystal works did not produce baubles. They made lenses for submarine periscopes.

The middle of the town consisted of a large square and a catholic church with a surrounding yard and cemetery. A tower, capped with the onion-like top so common in Tyrol and Bavaria, completed the picture of this alpine settlement. The two mountain ranges, north and south of Wattens, rose majestically to their snow covered peaks. The river Inn was grey in color and was almost ice-cold, even in high summer. It separated the valley from the abruptly rising mountains to the north. Only a few hundred meters between the river and town were some flat agricultural fields. The southern mountain range rose far less abruptly than its counterpart to the north. It was strewn with scattered farms and what appeared to be a secondary road. I later discovered that above this alpine idyll were the high pastures. Cattle would be taken up there for the entire summer and would not return to their barns until late fall.

On our arrival at the Cigarettenpapier Fabrik, an employee took us to our quarters. The rather large barrack-type building consisted of one large central room and two end rooms. One end room was occupied by a Viennese Austrian who had supposedly been kicked out of Vienna for political unreliability. He was an Austrian patriot and very much anti-Nazi. The middle room was occupied by Ukrainian women. They were forced laborers and had blue patches of cloth with the word OST (east) sewn on their blouses and outer coats. The last end room was to be ours. It had two-tier beds, a stove, and a sink. We entered and sat down. Our journey had ended. Here we would wait, completely ignorant of our future, for the end of the war, the restoration of Lithuanian independence, and our return home.

Chapter Five

The manager of the factory called on us several days later to see how we had settled in. On the left lapel of his jacket he wore a round insignia with a swastika in the center. This was the insignia of the Nazi party. He was a member of the National Socialist German Workers Party. By then I spoke a little German. He asked me what language I spoke at home. I was truthful and answered, "Nur litauisch". Only Lithuanian. Father probably cringed, but what else could I say. The plant manager was a pleasant type of a fellow despite being a Nazi.

The following Monday I was off to a local school. I entered fifth grade. The school itself was nice enough. The teachers were pleasant, even the one with the Nazi party insignia on her lapel. The kids were OK also. Even though I was not German I was tolerated, if not marginally accepted.

The very first day opened my eyes to the fact that learning a new language was not optional. The language was difficult, but with time I became able to communicate. When one is totally immersed in a foreign language, results become apparent rather quickly.

The subjects were taught somewhat differently from what I was used to. For example, back home we were taught world geography, but here the geography lessons only taught of Grossdeutschland. Math was OK, and I was quite comfortable with it.

The one really nice feature was lunch. It was either cooked on the premises or brought in and warmed up at the school. Either way it was plentiful and tasty.

Often, if there were few clouds and sunny, school was interrupted by the "Voralarm". Everyone was dismissed, and the idea was to go home as soon as possible.

Unlike school in Lithuania we used few copy books. We wrote, instead, on a Griffeltafel, a piece of slate set in a frame, with a hard, stone-like pencil. I once dropped and cracked my Griffeltafel. A permit had to be obtained before a stationary store would sell me a new one.

German punishment was heavy-handed compared to that in Lithuanian schools, where there was no corporal punishment. I think it was prohibited by law. Here, however, the use of the rod was common. If a kid got caught talking, he was told to come forward and lean over the teacher's desk, where he received at least two or three hits with a flexible rod.

Every Monday, school started with us singing the anthem of the Nazi Party, "Horst Wessel Lied", while giving the extended-arm Hitler salute. One time, a classmate next to me supported his right arm with his left. That was disrespectful to the highest degree. After the song, he had to present himself bent over at the teacher's desk. The teacher hit him so many times that it was, in effect, more of an assault and battery than enforcement of discipline. I can still recall the expression on the face of the Nazi bitch. To this day I wonder if she was not into sado-masochism.

Many years later, I discussed this incident with Father. He explained to me that many Austrians had been Nazis who wholeheartedly supported their compatriot, the Fuehrer. Austria had been a country that could not possibly lose the war. If Hitler had won, they would have considered themselves part of Germany. When Hitler lost, they told the world that they had been a neutral country occupied by Nazi Germany.

Days went on. One day did not differ from the next. I discovered from my parents that way back in the summer there had been an unsuccessful attempt on Hitler's life, that the Allies were advancing up the Italian peninsula, and that the Ardennes offensive, known in the United States as the Battle of the Bulge, had flopped. I was also told that new "wonder weapons" were being employed. The local newspaper and the weekly newsreel at the movies gave the impression that London had been reduced to a heap of rubble.

When school was not in session, Grandfather and I took walks around the surrounding areas. We found a beautiful waterfall. It was amazing to me as there were no waterfalls of any kind back home. Perplexed, I stood there and watched it.

One day, while we were returning from the waterfall, the siren sounded a Voralarm. Then it went into a panic-inducing, undulating shriek. This was the real alarm! Enemy battle formations were heading towards Innsbruck! Well, no one went into anything even resembling a panic. Wattens was some eighteen kilometers from Innsbruck. This was too far away for us to be bombed, even by mistake. Only once did a bomb fall into the surrounding fields, apparently because of some malfunction in a plane that had been crippled by flak or a fighter attack.

Although Innsbruck contained no great industrial targets, it was a rail center. From the east- west line a major trunk peeled off towards Brenner Pass and Italy. The German front in Italy was principally supported by this line. Therefore, air raids occurred daily if the weather was good.

That day was the usual show. From the vantage point of Swarovski works we watched the attack on Innsbruck unfold. The contrails, like gossamer tails, followed each silvery plane. The blue sky contrasted with the snowy engine exhaust of the planes. Flak smudges were in the sky even before the American formation got there. German Me-109s vanished, the pilots not wanting to fly into an area where their own flak could shoot them down. B-17s gleamed in the sunlight of the cloudless sky. To a kid who had only once before seen a four engine plane, the sheer enormity of the numbers was overwhelming. The airplane motors were quite loud, and the sound of flak bursts could be made out, though the distance muffled them.

Did any of this instill fear in me? Not in the least. Grandfather was trying to get me to go into the Swarovsky mine, which is where the local population sought shelter during air raids, but there was no power on earth that, at the moment, could get me inside and miss the aerial goings on.

In about thirty minutes the sky show was over and we started walking home. The all-clear sounded by the time we approached the factory gates. These events happened on a Sunday in either late November or early December. The town and the entire Alpine panorama were sparkling, covered by recent snowfall.

When Grandfather and I entered our quarters, we found a great surprise. Uncle Victor, Aunt Bernice, and little Jolanta had arrived from St Poelten, a town just west of Vienna. They were not part of the convoy crowd. I did not even know they had left Lithuania.

It quickly became obvious, even to me, that Uncle Victor had deserted the Red Army and under no circumstances could fall into Russian hands. Father criticized his brother for pulling such a surprise. Uncle Victor implied that with his brother's help he could find work, either at the cigarette paper factory or at Swarovski's. Uncle Victor was right. Swarovski hired him, and his family found a room at Gasthaus Zum Tiroler. Twenty-five years later, while visiting Wattens with Helaine and some other friends, I found the place to be externally unchanged, though the name was now Pension Zum Tiroler.

Winter in Tyrol was not very cold, but there was much snow. I saw some local kids with very nice sleds. I really wanted to acquire one! There was no place to buy one because of the war. Then I thought I had a stroke of luck. A rather fat employee of the factory said he could get me one. My hopes went up. I waited. Days became weeks. The sled never materialized. Eventually, the Foehn, a very warm wind from the south, arrived, signaling the end of winter. The sled was no longer needed.

That year, 1944, was our first Christmas away from home. I don't recall a Christmas tree, but I am sure we had one. Kucios, however, was very austere. It was held at Uncle Victor's. Compared to the previous Kucios in Sirviai, this was a melancholy affair. We all hoped to celebrate the next Christmas at home.

The following day was nice and sunny. At ten o'clock the Voralarm sounded, followed by the full alarm at eleven. This was accompanied by with the aerial show that by then was familiar to us. War did not take time off for Christmas.

A few weeks later, the alarm sounded at night. That was quite unusual. We heard airplanes, and their noise was much louder than usual. They sounded much lower than the day time formations. Carefully, Father drew the blackout curtains open. Outside, the sky was full of flares. They slowly descended in groups that looked like Christmas trees. The entire valley was so lit up that one could see the mountains on both sides. Then the flak started. Unlike the smudges we saw in daylight, each burst was a visible explosion. The sky was full of noise and fireworks. We were witnessing our first night air raid.

I noticed some peculiarities. The flak bursts seemed all to occur at the same altitude. During a daylight raid, flak smudges were spread over various altitudes. Daylight raid bomber formations were stacked in boxes at different heights. In the night raid, a stream of bombers flew at the same altitude.

Over Innsbruck, the searchlights moved all over the sky looking for a target for the flak. The planes were too far away from Wattens for us to tell if the searchlight efforts produced any results.

The next morning, in school, we were told that the previous night's raid had been carried out by the British. It had been a real terror attack. Instead of unloading their ordnance on the rail junction, they had dumped it all on Hungerburg, a quiet suburb of Innsbruck devoid of any military significance. That night, Hungerburg had been taken right off the map, with all the concomitant civilian slaughter that the raid entailed.

At this point, the last of our food from Sirviai was gone. We were reduced to eating dried bread that was soaked, formed into "pancakes", and fried. I remember the taste! You had to be very, very hungry to eat those "pancakes". Well, we were very, very hungry.

Mother, Aunt Bernice, and I went into the countryside to try and barter whatever cigarettes we had left for food. We had varied success. Some farmers were interested, while others were not. Sometimes, we'd come home with bread flour or other edible articles. Once, and only once, we got a piece of very good bacon!

Our dinner always came from the factory cafeteria, which was not known for its culinary prowess. But, of course, the staff did their best to prepare an edible hot meal. The most frequent dish they served was goulash. Well, it was called goulash. It didn't look, smell, or taste anything like what the name implied. It consisted of a few potatoes in a non-descript gravy-like liquid. Bread came with it, also. On one occasion we even had smoked herring. Now that was good. I have always liked smoked fish.

Ration cards allowed mother to buy certain additional items. On Sundays she was able to get white bread! Most of the time, however, we were just on the verge of being hungry.

Grandfather had his own particular problem. All the years I knew him he was a human tobacco incinerator. I was told he'd rather smoke than eat. I recall him in his study in Kaunas. He would be going over various briefs in the light of a Bank of England lamp. On one side of him was an elaborately inlaid cigarette box, on the other a large ashtray. Invariably, at the end of the evening the box was empty and the ashtray full.

By this point in our travels, all of the cigarettes we had brought from Kaunas were long gone. Grandfather started looking for a tobacco substitute. He began buying herbal teas. Those that appeared most similar to tobacco were rubbed, rolled in cigarette paper, and smoked. Good quality cigarette paper was in ample supply. After all, we lived on the grounds of a cigarette paper factory.

As I recall, the best herb tea for smoking was called Madras. This brand was smoked until the war ended. At this point American soldiers were in Wattens. They dropped cigarette butts all over, but most prodigiously along the main highway running through the center of town. It became my job to collect these butts and bring them to Grandfather. He disassembled them and rolled new cigarettes from the salvaged tobacco.

Two and half years later he was dead of lung cancer. Maybe that was the main reason I never smoked.

One overcast day, when the clouds were almost down to the valley floor, Mother decided to go shopping in Innsbruck. With such overcast there was no chance of an air raid. Of course, there were no centralized weather forecasts because of the war.

We boarded an early local for Innsbruck and arrived at about nine a.m. The station area of the city had been leveled by repeated bombings. A barrack served as the passenger terminal. All around us was a bizarre landscape. Bomb craters had railroad cars in them; one contained a locomotive. Rails reached up perpendicularly like strands of spaghetti. Various cables hung in Gordian tangles from the remaining electric towers. Rows and rows of new rails and concrete ties had been neatly stacked for the repair of future damage. Prisoners of some sort, under armed guard, were doing the repair work. And through this surreal landscape trains were moving! Trains loaded with tanks, guns, and troops headed south towards Brenner Pass. Others with Red Cross signs, loaded with wounded, moved in the opposite direction. Feldgendarmerie, as well as ordinary police, were present on the remains of the platform.

Mother was looking for a certain antique shop she said was on the other side of the river Inn. We started walking, through streets bordered by bombed-out buildings, towards an area that was minimally damaged. After a thirty minute walk, we approached a bridge and started to cross.

Suddenly, at both ends of the bridge, police car alarms sounded and blue lights flashed. The vehicles came to a screeching halt, and men, clad in leather coats, rapidly piled out of them and closed off both ends of the bridge. Leather coats were usually worn by Gestapo plainclothesmen. To me the coats represented a uniform of sorts, although ordinary civilians were occasionally seen in them.

These squads established a barrier and proceeded to check ID papers and the "Arbeitskarte", a certificate of current employment. No one was detained. Mother had her Arbeitskarte because she was employed as the supervisor of the Ukrainian women's living quarters.

The skies began to clear and the sun broke through the dissipating overcast. A few minutes later, sirens started to wail the full alarm. We hadn't heard the "Voralarm" as we had been on the train when it sounded. Mother inquired about the location of the nearest shelter. It turned out to be about ten minutes away in a specially dug cave in the mountain side.

Flak opened up as soon as we reached the vicinity of the shelter. The sound of the flak combined with the noise from the bomber engines and, shortly thereafter, bomb explosions from down in the city near the rail yards. Shrapnel began to fall, but by then we had entered the shelter. This communal cave was filled with women, children, infants in baby carriages, and an assortment of men, mostly of older age groups. The cacophony outside began to subside in about twenty minutes, and in about another half-hour the all-clear sounded.

"This was a short one," an old man near us remarked as we started towards the daylight of the exit. Short or not, this was my first and, fortunately, only air raid in which we were directly involved. I was scared big time. This was not like watching the show from the safety of Wattens.

My enthusiasm for shopping had been completely wiped out, but Mother continued looking for the antique shop. When we found it, business was being conducted as though nothing had happened. Such stoicism surprised me to no end.

The shop was known for old mother of pearl cameos, but I was fascinated by the old desks, chairs, oil paintings and various bronze and marble statues. Mother picked out a pearl cameo of a fisherman standing by his boat, and a bronze statue of a successful mountain hunter carrying a chamois on his shoulders. Both of these objects d'art have been standing on a bookshelf in our family room since Mother's death in 2002.

At last we made for the railroad station. As we got closer, evidence of the raid increased. Fire brigades were putting out fires. Prisoners were manually removing obstructions from the street we were walking on. Any easily found casualties had already been removed. Crews looked for other injured under the ruins. The sky was nearly cloudless, and the sun was way past its high point for the day.

Mother hoped there would be a train back to Wattens. It was a long, long walk home and any hotels that were still standing were reserved for important Nazis. The communal shelters were not very appealing, though if we needed to we could go to one for something to eat and a place to sleep.

To our happy surprise, the barrack at the station was intact, as were the rails in the immediate vicinity. In the distance, a multitude of people worked like ants as they filled in bomb craters, replaced rails, and removed various obstructions. Mother went into the barrack to inquire about trains going east. She was told that the local would be moving east towards Wattens as soon as the Berlin-Rome express went through. Before she could ask when that would be, the station official wrote on a black board "Berlin-Rome express 120 minutes late."

We went outside and found a place to sit and wait for our ride home. It was three or four hours since the last bomb had exploded. A few tracks away a train carrying tanks rolled towards Brenner. Mother took out two bread and margarine sandwiches. They were so tasty!

While eating them, I noticed two men wearing German army uniforms and turbans. That was totally incomprehensible. Turbans meant Indians. Why were the Indians here? What were they doing in these uniforms? By then I understood that Germany was fighting damn near the whole world. I also knew who the German allies were. But Indians! Wasn't India a colony of Great Britain? As these men passed us, I noticed their shoulder patches: "Freies Indien". Free India. The word "Freies" was being used as an adjective, not a verb.

It took many years and much reading of the history of World War Two before this enigma was solved for me. During the war, India had a small, organized independence movement devoted to obtaining India's total independence from the UK. Because the Indian army had divisions in the Western Desert, it is reasonable to assume that some of the soldiers became German prisoners of war. The Germans convinced some of these prisoners to turn against their colonial oppressors. These individuals never saw combat and were used only for purposes of propaganda.

At last our train came and we returned home. It was already dark when we arrived. I remember this day every year. It was April 20, 1945. Hitler's birthday.

The last of snow melted, and the weather became warmer each day. For the Germans it was evident the Thousand Year Reich had only a few weeks left. The town's Nazis were even more arrogant than usual. They spoke of new wonder weapons! Wait until the Fuehrer lets loose with them! Any talk of Germany's defeat was considered treason

Father cautioned Uncle Victor to be careful when expressing his views about the state of the war. My uncle, however, had difficulty keeping his mouth shut about the subject. All that was necessary was for some co-worker to repeat what he heard Victor Gamziukas say. The story would get to a party member, and then the well-oiled machinery of the Gestapo would go into gear. Grandfather, like my father, was very pragmatic. He knew that Hitler's jig was up, but kept it to himself.

One late afternoon, I saw a twin-engine aircraft approach Wattens in complete silence. I looked at it and was completely perplexed. Why were the two engines silent? The plane was infinitely faster than any other I had seen. When it was well past where I stood, I was overcome by a noise that followed the jet-propelled Me262. I had never heard this noise before. It sounded as though an entire squadron of conventional fighters had just passed over my head. In the distance, the jet went into a steep climb and disappeared over the northern mountain range.

I promptly described what I saw to Grandfather. He calmly explained that it could not have been Luftwaffe as Germany no longer had any aircraft. I thought Grandfather was not being entirely realistic.

After a few days, word spread through the town that the Americans were already in Innsbruck. Wehrmacht and Waffen SS moved in an orderly fashion east through the town square. German order was preserved, even in retreat.

Occasionally, MPs stopped vehicles and checked people's march orders. I was standing on a brick fence of the churchyard and had a very good view of the military checkpoint. The head hunters looked very business-like, methodical, and thorough. Behind every checker stood an SS man with a Schmeisser machine pistol slung across his chest. Soon, word got out that the SS was setting up a roadblock with antitank weapons, just west of the town. By now, however, the sun had set and dusk was enveloping Wattens. I hadn't been home for some time. It would be wise, I thought, to go home and face the music.

That night we all slept without any disruptions. Morning came and things were still quiet. After breakfast, I started for school knowing full well that it would probably be cancelled. In the town square, a strange-looking car with a canvas roof was parked under a linden tree. On its hood and sides was a white star inside a white circle. At that time I had no idea the vehicle was a Jeep. Two soldiers, in uniforms I had never seen before, stood near it conversing with a few locals. I made my way toward this interesting scenario. One of the soldiers spoke fluent German with a local cop. His companion occasionally interrupted him in a language totally new to me. Well, I knew that Americans were coming, and that the language in America was English, so I figured out that these were the Americans. Therefore, I knew I was hearing English, without understanding a single word.

Out of the corner of my eye, I noticed two German soldiers carrying rifles slung from their shoulders. These two were at the other end of the square, perhaps 150 yards away. The adversaries noticed each other at about same time. Now what? Would there be a shooting? It was not to be. The Americans did not go for their guns, and the Germans discretely disappeared down a side street. Common sense had prevailed.

By the end of the day, many American vehicles had moved through the town. What happened to the fight to the death at the SS road block? Rumors circulated that the mayor of the town had had the brains and guts to go and talk to the commander of Hitler's heroes. Apparently, even they had seen the futility of trying to stop General Mark Clark's armies.

There were no more air raids. Street lights came back on. But life was far, far from normal. School was out, so the very good school lunches became a pleasant memory. Our food situation in general was becoming acute.

Despite our hunger, the immediate aftermath of the war was very interesting. The field across the road from where we lived was now filled with Italian tanks and self-propelled German assault guns. They appeared overnight. I had no idea who had parked them there. No one was guarding them, however, and in a course of a day they became my private property for exploration. I would climb into an Italian tank, elevate and lower the gun, traverse the turret, and make like I was using the machine gun. It was good that whoever had transported this military theme park here had made sure that all the ammunition was removed.

At about same time, the town swimming pool opened. I would swim until my teeth chattered from the cold water. Then I'd walk over to the "tank park" and get inside one of the steel machines to warm up. By about three in the afternoon, the sun would heat up the hull and turret like an oven. I have no idea how high the inside temperature actually became, but my teeth would stop chattering in next to no time.

As days went by, other Wattens Lithuanians began to appear, as if they were answering a summons. Grandfather's colleague, Judge Kalvaitis, was the first to arrive. Next was a fellow by the name of Zeleniakas, who showed up with his family. This individual was quite a piece of work! He had a British passport! He had carried it through the collapsing Reich, passing through numerous Gestapo spot checks and acquiring many travel permits, but neither his luggage nor his body had ever been searched. At this point, I don't think that I have to explain what his fate would have been if the Gestapo had gotten a whiff of the British document.

It was Zeleniakas that introduced himself to the local American commanding officer and explained to him that the town had a number of

Lithuanian refugees. The local CO was a very kind man who offered us food to supplement our diet. Speak of manna from heaven! Our hunger stopped at this point. The local factory-employee Nazis became very deferential to us when the word got out we were getting food from the victorious Americans.

I must have been a real wise-guy in those days. A one-armed plant supervisor, who had always worn his NSDAP button and expected me to greet him every morning with an enthusiastic "Heil Hitler", was nowhere to be seen. One morning, however, we almost ran into each other while rounding a corner. "Heil Hitler, Herr Dschek," I said to him. Then, most insolently, I continued, "Jetzt Ich bin hoeher als Sie." Directly translated this means "now I'm higher than you." I never saw this Party member again. He may have disappeared into the denazification system.

Zeleniakas' son, some 20 years old, managed to get himself a car. The car, a relatively new Adler with front wheel drive, was simply requisitioned from a Wattens Nazi. Accompanied by an American lieutenant, the son simply went to the Nazi's home and came back driving the car. The member of the Party was apparently overjoyed that the ami (American) wanted just his car and not him. Soon, I was riding around town in this fine cabriolet. My school acquaintances must have been flabbergasted to see me in the car. One day young Zeleniakas even asked me if I wanted to drive his convertible. I thought I wasn't hearing right. In just a minute, I was behind the wheel with the car moving. I did, however, have trouble reaching the accelerator with my foot. After all, I was only eleven and half years old.

Between these exhilarating interludes, I spent a lot of time walking along the main highway trying to find American cigarette butts for Grandfather. I noticed other kids, and even adults, doing the same thing. Competition was growing. But there were enough for all of us. Americans were world-class smokers and always left good-sized butts behind.

One day, while I was observing large lizards in a discarded rag pile, an unknown kid who was about my age approached me. His name turned out to be Grabnickas, and his family lived in the environs of Wattens. I think his family lived on the Fritzens side of the river Inn. This was a fantastic surprise. A kid my age who spoke Lithuanian! An immediate friendship developed that lasted from our time in Augsburg to more than thirty years later when he owned a motel in Lake Wales, Florida. In 1979 we had a reunion of the Augsburg high school alumni in his hotel. The dear friend died on his daughter's wedding day in 1982. A sad epilogue for a friendship that started that beautiful day in Tyrol.

News reached us that the Americans were leaving, and French army would be arriving to take their place. To me this was confounding. What were the French doing posing as victors? They lost the war! After throwing in the towel, they had a German-formed government! One of their national heroes had become Hitler's marionette as French head of state. Many times, when I listened to an adult discussion of world politics, I heard Father refer to France as the sick, old woman of Europe. As I grew in years, education, and common sense, I realized how correct Father was. Nonetheless, here they were, the conquering frogs. Some individuals said that Frenchies were grabbing people off the streets of Innsbruck, hauling them off to their military hospital, and draining a unit of blood before releasing them. Oh, the glorious, victorious French. Years later I visited France on several occasions. My impression of their country was that if I never visited it again it would not be too soon.

Sometime in the early summer a letter arrived from Petokas, one of the members of the original exodus convoy. He and several other convoy members were in a displaced persons camp in Augsburg, under the auspices of UNRRA (United Nations Refugee Relief Administration). His letter was very emphatic. "Come to Augsburg! Most of the convoy crowd is already here. There are Lithuanians numbering in the hundreds. The other Balts are also well represented. What are you going to do, stay in the French zone of occupation in Austria?" Well, this letter motivated the Wattens Lithuanians to come together and make a decision. Should we stay or go? The decision to go won overwhelmingly.

There was a problem, however. In this early post-war period the passenger trains were not running! Augsburg was not the next town. It was in the next country. Austria was now posturing as an innocent neutral.

An individual by the name of Vizgirda informed those gathered in our room that it was possible to rent a freight car. Where? How? Everyone was full of questions about this proposition. "In Innsbruck," Vizgirda asserted. Well, everyone agreed that this should be pursued. Vizgirda, it turned out, was Aunt Bernice's brother-in-law and lived in Innsbruck. The next day he went to the offices of Deutsche Reichs Bahn (German RR). Several days later Vizgirda returned and not only informed us that he had rented a freight car, but gave us a departure date and time as well. We would leave Innsbruck at four p.m. on a specific day in June. I cannot recall the actual date.

Father inquired about the route of this "magic" freight train. Well, that was a little more complicated. The train would go as far as Kufstein. After that we would have to contact the station master to have our car coupled to a train traveling to Munich. "A-ha," said Father, "Then what?" Well, then the trip would become almost like hitch-hiking on the railroad.

On the appointed day, we gathered all of our meager possessions, got on a gas generator truck, and set off for Innsbruck. In the marshalling yard, an official directed the truck towards the freight train that would take us out of Tyrol. We were all excited to be returning to the country where the sun sets at a distant horizon. None of us had seen our usual kind of sunset for many months. I had a very distinct longing for wide horizons. I guess one has to be born in the mountains to always accept a late sunrise and an early sunset.

We found the train and our assigned carriage. Everything was transferred from the wheezy truck to the freight car. The owner of the truck was paid, after which he stoked the gas generator and departed for home at the top speed of twenty kilometers per hour. At precisely four o'clock, with a lot of banging of coupled cars and the screeching of wheels grinding against the rails, the train started out of the marshalling yard. About a half-hour later we were rolling through the tiny Wattens depot. The town looked like a Tyrolean postcard. I did not feel any nostalgia or loss. It was just a phase in our journey away from the Bolsheviks. I felt like we were off to another country, another adventure.

At the age of eleven, I had no idea that in a distant future my oldest daughter would be playing a violin made in Wattens.

Chapter Six

Late in the evening, when we were getting ready to make some sleeping arrangements right on the floor of the freight car, the train started to slow down. Soon we saw lights in the distance and what appeared to be a marshalling yard. Just like in Innsbruck, the terrain was pocked with bomb craters, the remains of railroad buildings, and wrecked rolling stock. This had to be Kufstein. I fell asleep using a small bundle of our belongings as a pillow. I slept without feeling any movement of the train or people around me. A freight car is not exactly a Wagon Lit of the Compagnie Internacionale. It isn't a Pullman. But that night I was dead to the world.

When I woke up, there were no more mountains. Rolling countryside extended to the horizon on both sides of the train. Church steeples were scattered through the landscape. Their onion-tops stuck out among the surrounding red-roofed houses. Lush green fields extended into the distance.

Strangely, the train was slowing down. There was no marshalling yard in sight. No city or town. And yet, it continued at a slower pace for what seemed like several hours. Again, we traveled through bombed-out areas. People were all over, working like ants to repair the damage of the war. When the train finally stopped, we discovered from the workmen that this was Rosenheim. The train was shoved abruptly forward and backward, and I concluded that changes were being made in the makeup of our train. Some freight cars were disconnected, and new ones were attached. After a relatively short time, our journey continued.

When the landscape later started to change from rural to suburban, Father remarked that we were entering Munich. I knew precisely where Munich was, what rivers flowed through it, and what other cities were near it. I knew these things because I had always liked to look at maps. Any maps. Atlases, maps of countries, continents and cities. This habit stayed with me my entire life.

As the train decelerated, a clearer picture of Munich appeared. I had never seen so large an area so completely converted into ruins. Much later, while reading about strategic bombing in World War Two, I discovered that 50% of Munich had been destroyed.

After about an hour of moving at reduced speed, we came to stop in what was left of a huge marshalling yard. Two tracks over was another train full of people in an assortment of tattered military uniforms. Apparently, these were liberated prisoners of war, but they really looked like barbarians of some sort. From the shape of their hats I could tell these were Serbs going home. Their freight cars were decorated with chalk drawings of various communist symbols: hammer and sickles, five-pointed stars, and inscriptions in the Cyrillic alphabet. One had to be a complete moron not to recognize the predominant political philosophy of these passengers.

At one point Uncle Victor shouted, surprising everyone in our car. "Look," he yelled, "there's a carriage of The Lithuanian State Rail Road". Almost directly in front of us was a wooden freight car with an extraordinary designation on it: Lietuvos Gelzkelis. Everybody became silent. Then Grandfather said, "It made it through all the bombs, fires, and explosions, never to return home." This simple phrase of his described quite accurately the passengers in our own carriage. This beat-up box car was the last visual reminder of home we saw.

The trains were opposite one another. The noisy Serbs showed little concern for the presence of women among us. They answered nature's calls without any concerns of modesty. There were no conversations between us and them. Their communist graffiti precluded any exchange.

After a while we heard the banging between coupled cars that meant the train was starting. Apparently, Munich was not its final destination. Augsburg was only a short ride away, but we had a long wait on a siding somewhere between the two cities. We didn't arrive in Augsburg until the next morning.

When the train stopped, several carriages, including ours, were disconnected and taken to a smaller yard in Hochfeld. The tracks traveled between many intact five-story buildings. These edifices appeared to be fully occupied. There were many kids on the street between the rail yard and the homes. One of the kids shouted, in our native tongue, "Are you Lithuanian?" Eventually, the tiny locomotive stopped. Our journey from Wattens to Augsburg was over.

Since there was no point of staying in the car any longer, we assembled our possessions, climbed down from our home of quite a few days, and went out to the street.

I was standing alone and behind the rest of the new arrivals when I noticed a boy my age making his way towards me. Not us as a group, but towards me personally! As he got closer I recognized him. It was the same Algis Grabnickas who had visited us in Wattens. An animated exchange followed, and Algis filled me in about this place. He lived in the building directly behind us. The other inhabitants were also Lithuanian. As a matter of fact, there were some 1100 compatriots! The rest were other Balts and some Ukrainians. This was a DP camp. A displaced person camp.

As Algis and I were talking, Father called me over and explained that he and I were going to another DP camp where our living quarters were supposedly waiting for us. Grandfather and the others were to wait in a sort of community barrack.

We set off for the streetcar going to Haunstetten. After entering the street named Haunstettenstrasse, we immediately saw an approaching streetcar. Father and I ran for the stop. I could not keep up with him. He took off like a scared cat, and I lagged way behind. However, neither one of us made it to the stop in time to catch the streetcar. We resigned us to waiting. After the war Innsbruck streetcars showed up at completely random intervals. After one passed the next might take an hour to show up.

While we were wondering how long we would have to wait, a streetcar light appeared in the distance. It was the No.4, going to the suburb of Haunstetten. After boarding we noticed that the car ran on a track next to the highway. The tracks and the highway ran through an open country. The stops were mainly at various Messerschmitt works and the company's main administration building. There were few dwellings between where we got on and the suburb of Haunstetten. Ultimately, the conductor announced, "Protestantische Kirche!" With a great screeching of wheels, the streetcar rounded the Protestant church and came to a stop.

After getting off, Father inquired as to where Fink Srasse was. The local told us how to get there and added that it was now in an area inhabited by "Auslaender". Foreigners! We walked for about half an hour. Then, in the distance, we saw three flagpoles, each with a Baltic flag gently waving in a light summer breeze. This was the place.

Chapter Seven

A predominant language did not exist in the administration barracks. Many people spoke Lithuanian, but their conversations were sometimes drowned out by heavily accented German. German was spoken between Estonians and other Balts. I heard Russian as well. That was somewhat of a surprise! I soon learned, however, that Russian was the only practical language for communicating with the Ukrainians. Ukrainians hated the Ruskis as much as we Lithuanians, but for practical reasons the lingo had to be used.

A self-important looking individual walked into the barracks. He wore an American uniform that had no American insignia. Who was this peacock? Well, closer examination of his American-style uniform revealed a shoulder patch that said "UNRRA" (United Nation Refugee Relief Administration). Everybody present was very deferential to this personage.

At this point, an old friend of Father's named Tursa walked in. The two of them got into a long conversation while I sat and watched the comings and goings of the administration building.

A truck was acquired. We drove back to Hochfeld, picked up everyone who had been sharing the railroad freight car from Innsbruck, and returned to Rechenstrasse 56, Haunstetten. To be complete in the terms of those times I should also add "Germany, US Zone". The last phrase was colloquially referred to as the "American Zone". It was called that for a few years until the name was changed to the Federal Republic of Germany. I imagine that even then it took a few months to drop this war remnant.

We were assigned an attic apartment. Uncle Victor and his family had one room. Grandfather slept in the kitchen. The rest of my family stayed in what was the parlor when the original inhabitants had lived there.

Thus we became DP's and took up residence in the DP Camp.

It would be negligent not to enlighten the reader of the postwar situation in western Germany and the phenomenon of the displaced person. After the Ribbentrop-Molotov Pact, the Russians occupied Lithuania. Deportations, incarcerations, and the just plain murder of well-to-do farmers, intelligentsia, and other influential persons caused some 200,000 Lithuanians to emigrate to the west. This migration involved all the Balts and other eastern-European nationalities. In addition to these, there were hundreds of thousands of forced labor workers that had been brought from their occupied lands to work in the German war plants. All of these people were now free. Some went home, and others stayed in the west, where they felt it was safer.

All these displaced people now lived in camps of mixed nationalities. The word camp is used loosely. There were no tents or woods. With the authority given by the occupying powers, the UNRAA requisitioned sections of towns and cities. They requisitioned former German military barracks (Caserne). Local German population was evicted from their homes. Millions of people who had left their countries due to the onslaught of the Red Army were channeled into these locales. To my knowledge there were no serious frictions between the DP ethnic groups, at least not in Augsburg. Initially, these camps were administered and logistically supported by UNRRA. Later, however, the name was changed to the International Refugee Organization (IRO).

Eventually, resettlement meant the end of the system. There was a time period when there were forced repatriations. Ukrainians suffered the most. They were simply shipped home by force. Knowing the persecution that awaited them, many committed suicide. None of the Balts were subjected to this violation of human rights. But those were tense weeks. Everyone wondered if they would be next.

As these events illustrate, the West was talking out of both sides of its mouth. They liberated Europe from Hitler, gave all of Eastern Europe to Stalin, and now, with complete disregard of much vaunted human rights, returned Ukrainians to certain slavery or death in the depths of Siberia. These repatriations stopped with the beginning of the Berlin Air Lift, where the West finally clarified its position in regards to the East. While the West was trumpeting the great liberation, we Lithuanians came to understand that our country would again be under Bolshevik occupation, and we would never see our homeland free again. The three grand leaders decreed so at Yalta!

Life in a DP camp was a challenge for the adults. Most, like my parents and Grandfather, were educated elite. Most had held high positions of responsibility as university professors, corporate executives, physicians, attorneys, etc. Now they were unemployed and no better than the minimally educated individual that had been drafted into the German anti-aircraft corps or had been grabbed off the street in Kaunas and brought to Germany for labor. They lost all of their property. Homes, farms, and businesses had been left behind for the communists to dispose of as they saw fit. Extremely few had a foreign bank account. Most had been separated from close relatives they might never see again. There were no jobs. The German economy, like its cities, was a pile of rubble. But even if the economy had been minimally OK, the poor language skills of the exiles precluded meaningful employment.

Life, however, did not stagnate. A theater group and a choir were soon formed. An Augsburg Lithuanian newspaper began publishing on a weekly basis. Former teachers, of whom we had quite a few, organized a grammar school and gymnasium. Not a gymnasium in an American sense, but in the European sense of a university preparatory high school. Language courses, particularly English and French, became popular. There were no suicides, and depression was kept at bay. Those who had relatives in America started trying to establish contact with them, hoping for help from overseas. Older teenagers entered German universities, and recent university graduates went for advanced degrees. My Uncle Albert Tarulis acquired a Ph.D. in political science. This eventually landed him a job at what then was called Carnegie Tech (now Carnegie Mellon) in Pittsburgh. Slowly but surely, people showed signs of psychological survival. Life went on.

What happened to the indigenous people of the "Siedlung", as the Germans called the area? Well, when the Americans decided to make room for an ever-increasing numbers of refugees, as already mentioned, they simply told the locals to get out. They were thrown out and had to fend for themselves. Between the buildings where we lived were vegetable gardens planted by these people. From time to time we would see them come to harvest what they could. It really was a sorry situation. We left their gardens alone, but there is no doubt in anyone's mind that our presence was, justifiably, resented.

I found most of the kids who had traveled in our original convoy from Lithuania to East Prussia living in another DP camp, not in Haunstetten. Hochfeld was much more austere. The apartments were much bigger and shared by more families. The people were not issued rations; they either had to come to the dining hall to eat or carry hot food home with them.

In Haunstetten rations were distributed once a week. We picked them up, and it was up to us from then on. At first the food was mostly canned, with the exception of white bread from an American army bakery. I was not too fond of the bleached flour slices. They had minimal flavor and were very much like the Wonder Bread found in any supermarket in the States today. One could easily obtain vegetables from the local economy by bartering. For example, one can of corned beef for so many bunches of carrots, beets, lettuce, etc. In general, life in Haunstetten was much more pleasant than in Hochfeld and we soon were called "lords" by the Hochfeld Lithuanians. However, no one in either location went hungry. The story of the German population was another matter.

Several days after our arrival, some friends and I went to see downtown Augsburg. We took the number four streetcar all the way to Königsplatz, the center of the city. It had been known as Adolf Hitler Platz before the Thousand Year Reich went down the tubes. While still on the streetcar, we saw that the city consisted of empty building facades and ruins as far as the eye could see. The medieval town had been surrounded by walls at one time, but now only various gates remained. The streetcar passed Rotes Tor, the Red Gate. It was untouched by any bomb. Behind it stood a beautiful, renaissance-style church that shared a wall with a smaller church. At the time of this visit I knew nothing of Augsburg's history. Later, in school, I learned that this town was truly one of the pivotal centers of western civilization, particularly during the Reformation.

Augustana Vendelicorum was the Roman name for the city founded by Emperor Augustus in 17 BC. Later changed to Augsburg, it is the second oldest town in Germany today. The oldest is Trier, miles to the northwest from Augsburg. During the middle ages, Augsburg was the home of two prominent families: The Fuggers, of banking fame, and the Welsers, whose holdings included all of what is today's Venezuela. During the Reformation, Martin Luther stayed in the city under the protection of the Fuggers. It is interesting to note that the gymnasium I attended was located on Anna Platz; directly across from the church now known as Fugger Kapelle. Martin Luther lived here in a room built for the clergy. Confessio Augustana (The Augsburg Confession) took place here before a papal representative. Also, an end to religious wars was agreed upon in this city. This termination of hostilities became known as the Peace of Augsburg.

Augsburg is noted for being the home of the Renaissance artist Holbein the Elder and birthplace of Holbein the Younger. His home, along with so many other dwellings, fell victim to allied bombing. In modern times, the city may claim fame as the birth place of Rudolf Diesel and as the location of an airfield from which the first operational jet, the Me-262, took to the air. On the infamous side, Rudolf Hess, one of Hitler's cronies, took off from Augsburg when he flew to Scotland on a misconceived peace mission. It is interesting to observe that Munich was less than nothing when Augsburg was at its historic high point as the capital of Swabia. Then, some monks on the river Isar asked Augsburg for permission to establish and operate a ferry. Augsburg consented, and the rest is history.

Our first visit to the city was essentially a walk among the ruins. For block after block, streets had only narrow passageways zigzagging through the rubble. Here and there was a store that was open and doing business.

One such store was a camera shop. We saw two American soldiers walk in. We watched through the open door as they handled a Leica camera. They were obviously interested in buying it. One put a pack of Camel cigarettes on the counter. The proprietor motioned with his hands indicating "no deal." The soldier reached in his pocket and produced two more packs of the cigarettes. Using a mix of English and German, he informed the proprietor that it was either three packs or no deal. We were flabbergasted when the deal went through! For three lousy packs of Camels the guy walked out with a Leica! We were so naïve, so stupid, and so easily surprised. We had so much to learn of this new world we were in. But learn we did. And fast!

It was getting towards dinner time. After a brief walk to Königsplatz, we got on the number four street car and went home.

Food in our camp was plentiful but, as mentioned earlier, always canned or packaged in some other way. There was one particular item that even hungry DPs were not crazy about. I, however, loved this culinary wonder. It was simply called "vegetables and meat", and it came in a can perhaps a little bit bigger than the standard tuna can of today. I loved it so much that word spread through the Lithuanian colony that "this crazy kid loves the slop." Later, I learned to say, "de gustibus non disputandum est." We will not argue over the matter of taste.

The days going by were exciting, filled with new, interesting and wondrous discoveries. For example, once, while hiking through the nearby woods, we found a ditch full of discarded Wehrmacht (German army) weapons and equipment. There were new Schmeissers, Mauser rifles, pistols and revolvers of German and foreign make, and plenty of ammunition. The older kids knew how some of them worked, so soon the staccato of a Schmeisser and the single shots of a Parabellum 38 could be heard. When I look back on that scene, I am convinced that the Lord was watching over us. No one was hurt. However, our excited merry-making had been heard all the way in the village of Haunstetten. When we came back to this battlefront playground a few days later we found nothing. The local authorities must have realized that weaponry like that had to be removed in order to prevent a tragedy.

Not long thereafter, word got to us that at the Messerschmitt works airfield were planes that had been parked and abandoned. We had to check it out. We found a hole in a metal fence and found ourselves in an incredible playground, the likes of which very few kids had ever laid their eyes on. By then most of us could identify the Luftwaffe aircraft, and we recognized the neatly arranged Me-109's and Me-210's. Behind these were several flak towers with 20 mm "Vierlings" that had four 20mm cannon on the same gun mount. The Towers allowed flak to be fired over the roofs at any low-flying "Jabos" (allied fighter bombers).

As we ran in, the oldest of our gang announced, "Nobody climbs the flak towers!" This was a smart command. There had been nobody on the flak tower since the end of the war. Seeing kids there would certainly attract the village police, so we limited ourselves to examining the planes. That was a ball. I sat in the pilot's seat and imagined that I was participating in dogfight! One fifteen year old was much more practical than us twelve-year olds. He noticed that some Me-210's had a clock.

Well, we went back to the camp. Several screwdrivers were acquired, and we again made off for the airfield. I don't remember how many clocks we uninstalled, but airplane clocks were being sold at the community building that evening.

Somehow our ventures into the Luftwaffe graveyard remained undiscovered for quite some time, maybe a week or two. But then something happened that brought American MP's to the scene. One drizzly, grey morning an older kid by the name of Algis got into the cockpit of a Me-110. He pretended to be the pilot in a dogfight. He moved the control stick to cause imaginary movements of "his" plane. The plane, of course, was as stationary on the ground as a field stone. The props did not turn, but Algis was having a great time imagining himself to be a Luftwaffe ace. During these shenanigans, he accidentally flipped open a previously unnoticed cover on the control stick. Underneath the cover was a red button. He pressed it. To everyone's horror, the cannon in the nose of the aircraft began firing. Fortunately, there was a brick wall about a hundred meters in front of the aircraft. We saw the pock marks appear as the 20 mm rounds hit the wall. This lasted only a few seconds, but it gave all of us enough time to get out of any aircraft we were in and run for the hole in the fence, the "ace" trailing behind us.

We did not run directly for camp, but for the open fields and bushes not too great a distance from the fence. Then our gang crept slowly through the bushes until the distance between us and the airfield was about one kilometer. At this point we stepped onto a macadamized road and innocently walked back home, approaching the camp from the opposite direction.

When we arrived, the DP camp was abuzz about the shooting in the airfield. We, of course, knew nothing about it.

While moving through the bushes we had heard the sirens of American MP Jeeps. Our activities attracted more than the local German Polizei. This time the American military were involved. Just one day later, two local policemen, armed with double barrel shotguns, patrolled the fence. Word had it that their blunderbusses were loaded with rock salt. The Americans apparently did not trust the Germans with real ammunition this soon after the cessation of hostilities. Rock salt, however, was enough to keep us from ever returning to that wonderful playground.

During the late summer, we spent much time hiking and exploring the woods. To the east was a substantial forest. One or one and a half kilometers deep in the forest we found the river Lech. It was grey and murky, somewhat reminiscent of the river Inn. Well, the headwaters of this river were somewhere west of Innsbruck, in the Alps. That explained its appearance and why its water was so cold at this time of year. We went swimming in it, but no one could stay in the water for more than a few minutes. It was that cold. And this was late August, the time of year when lakes and rivers are the warmest! Also, on several occasions we tried fishing in the Lech, but had no success.

Due west of Haunstetten was another river, the Wertach. Its banks were overgrown with bushes and some trees, but the surrounding fields were farmland. The water in it was crystal clear. A series of shallow rapids and the occasional deep hole constituted the topography of the bottom. One fine afternoon we heard splashing in the water on the other side of the bushes. We carefully approached the scrub on the bank. To our great delight, we spied four local girls taking a swim. They were a magnificent sight to behold. They were so pretty! The sun shone though their hair and the water they splashed. Their girlish shrieks somehow excited me. All of them were so carefree. They were also completely naked! At this point, one of our gang rolled off the bank and with a great splash fell into the water. The nymphs were gone in less than a second. The urge to kill that slob was hard to control.

We spent many hours frolicking in the Wertach. The water, in addition to being clear, was usually comfortably warm, so much so that one spring we opened the swimming season on the twentieth of April, the Fuehrer's birthday. I even tried to swim in it in October on a warm autumn day. Man, that was surprise. It was colder than an icebox!

We also tried our hand at fishing the river. We saw fish in the deeper areas, but never caught any. We tried and tried, but just had no luck.

During our stay in Haunstetten, our gang found some square-shaped ponds containing northern pike. We caught minnows in the Wertacht. Using them as bait, we caught some pike.

While on our way home, a German forest guard on a bicycle caught up with the six of us. He promptly told us that we were "verhaftet" (arrested) and were to follow him as he walked, pushing his bike. I thought that this time we were in real trouble. The oldest kid, about sixteen years old, kept a conversational tone as he told us in Lithuanian, "Where this path enters the grove I will whistle. We all will take off in six different directions." He did not have to give any additional explanation. As soon as he whistled, I took off like the devil himself was after me. A dry branch scratched my face, but I survived. Just like the others, I made it home alone. The cop did not know who to go after. Besides, one could tell by his appearance that he was in no shape to chase anyone in the woods. The fish, however, remained tied to his bike. More than likely he had a great supper.

At the time it wasn't clear to us why we got arrested, but we never went anywhere near those square-shaped ponds again. Later, we discovered they were state owned fish hatcheries.

Autumn came. The world's lousiest autumn is in Augsburg. It did not rain much, but there were weeks of constant drizzle that turned everything unpaved into mud. Temperatures, although not freezing, required some sort of outer garment.

By then I had outgrown my Lithuanian clothing. Fortunately, the UNRRA started distributing used German army clothing. I got an overcoat that was much too big for me. Then they turned us loose in a room full of used mountain-troop shoes. They were black with hobnailed soles and fittings for skis. They were quite usable, but had a couple of problems. First, they were unpaired and second, they were loose. Well, I needed a larger pair of shoes for the winter because my shoes from home were getting pretty tight. With great resolution, I started searching for a shoe that fit my foot well and still had room to allow two pairs of socks in the winter time.

I found an acceptable right shoe. Now the task was to find the left one. Unfortunately, my labor yielded shoes that were either too big or too small. There were many other people who were also looking. They all appeared to be determined and aggressive, and the pile began to get noticeably smaller. I thought to myself *if you want two shoes, even if they don't match, you'd better get your rear end in gear!* I continued to pick up shoes that were too big or too small, but never found one that was just a *little* too long or too short. Eventually, I had to settle for a rather noticeable disparity, with one several centimeters longer than the other. At first I was always self conscious, but as time went by this feeling disappeared. "A dog gets used even to being hung," goes an old Lithuanian adage.

Right about this time the former teachers from Lithuania organized a gymnasium. To enter a given grade you either had to present a school certificate from home or take an exam for the grade you wished to enter. My parents had the necessary certificate for first year of a gymnasium, but they felt that I could pass the exam for second. So I sat for entry into second year. I was successful.

As previously mentioned, the gymnasium was on Anna Platz in the center of the city. To get there we took the number four street car to Königsplatz then walked a few short blocks to school. The curriculum followed the one prescribed by the Lithuanian government before the war. Many years later this curriculum was recognized by the educational authorities of the Federal Republic of Germany.

Most of my school mates in Haunstetten were either a grade above or a grade below me. I was the only one in the second class who lived in the camp of the "lords"; the rest of my classmates were from Hochfeld. Classes were held in the afternoon. This meant that I was the only one who took the number four street car back to Haunstetten when the fifth period ended. I also had to walk alone from the car stop to the camp, which was a considerable distance away. I've never forgotten how miserable I felt walking the dark streets of the village in an autumn drizzle. No one from Haunstetten was ever added to the second class. The Hochfeld kids always traveled in a gang, having a ball wherever they went. I was very envious of their social group. Being alone reminded me of being back in Wattens.

One particularly nasty October afternoon, I returned from school and found an American soldier sitting on the bed in the main room of the apartment. That was a great surprise. Who? Why? These were the first thoughts that flashed through my head. "Hello," he said to me. I knew absolutely no English. Not knowing what to say, I repeated his greeting. At this point I saw Grandfather sitting at the table and writing something voluminous judging by the number of pages he had already filled.

Mother walked in and explained that this was Walter Brazer, the son of Grandfather's brother in America. Apparently, one of several letters that Grandfather had sent to America had reached his brother. That, in itself, was a small wonder as the Brazers had moved several times during the early forties. One of these moves had not been just a change of streets; it had been a move from Medina to Buffalo. Young Brazer had fought with the American army until the end of the war and was now waiting to be shipped home. His father wrote to him and told him to find us.

The second small miracle was his successful search for us in the immediate post war Germany. Years later, when we were in Buffalo, I questioned him about his arrival at Rechenstrasse 56. His story demonstrates how a persistent individual can prevail, even without knowing the local language.

Walter waited until grandfather finished his long correspondence. Mother offered him what meager food we had, which he ate unceremoniously. He gave us many canned items and chocolate, and to me he gave chewing gum. That was great. It was a status symbol to walk around chewing gum. When it was getting dark he took Grandfather's letter, put on his army great coat, bid us good luck, and disappeared into the gloom of Bavarian autumn evening. The next time we saw him was in Buffalo Central Terminal on a very hot Fourth of July, 1949. This visit was the beginning of a great effort to emigrate to the States.

Although the two DP camps shared a gymnasium, we were otherwise apart in our social lives. This was especially noticeable in the summer. They stuck to the city; we stuck to the outdoors.

On rainy days we spent our time on ping-pong and got quite good at it. Sometimes we played for hours on end. Even the mediocre became at least average. Now it appears funny. When I was a medical student, many years later, there were only two other ping-pong aficionados in the entire school of medicine that I couldn't beat. And one of them was a resident physician! He therefore had much more time to hone his skills than a third-year student.

Winter or summer, whenever the sun was shining we were in the woods. In the winter we would just plain hang out with the gang, but always away from the town. In the summer the two rivers were our playground. Fishing, swimming, and cooking our own soup on the banks of the Lech made us real outdoorsmen. I developed a love of the outdoors that carried into my adult live.

By the late spring of 1946 the Lithuanian scout movement had been resurrected throughout the DP camps of West Germany. I could not wait to become a scout. The ideals and methods of Lord Baden Powell were most appealing to me and the rest of the Lithuanian kids. Soon we swore the oath and became scouts. Girls, in similar fashion, became guides. Hanging out in the woods became organized into purposeful scout hiking, camping, and skill development. We soon acquired the knowledge described in the book "Scouting for Boys". All of us became proficient in taking care of ourselves in the wild. Later in my life, whether I was hunting in Western New York State or canoeing in Canada, I always remembered that I learned these skills as a scout in Haunstetten. As a matter of fact, I was aghast when I later discovered how little the average American Boy Scout knew of the outdoors.

The methodology of our learning was at the root of this difference. Our scout masters were adults who had spent their entire lives in scouting, acquiring skills from learning and experience. They had done the things mentioned in Baden Powell's book. They taught us by actual demonstration. This was very useful. There is nothing in any of life's endeavors that is successful without skills acquired hands-on.

In the fall of 1946, I became aware that mother was expecting. We still lived on Rechenstrasse. We were informed that another apartment would be available on Flachsstrasse the following January. This would be about the time mother was due. It would be just for Grandfather and our family. Uncle Victor's family would also move to Flachsstrasse, but a block away.

The winter of 1946/47 was very cold; it was later declared the coldest in some fifty years. We received notification to move on January 14th. On that day mother went into labor. She was admitted into an upscale private obstetrical clinic, and my sister Maria was born.

On returning from the maternity facility, Father announced that we would begin the move. It was a very cold midwinter day, but it was not accompanied by snow or high winds. It took many trips to move even our very limited possessions.

The apartment on the first floor of Flachsstrasse 32 consisted of a bedroom, a common kitchen and living room, and a small corridor with a bathroom on the street side. It was a bathroom without a bath. The adjoining housing project for the Messerschmitt works employees looked very complete on the outside, but such amenities as bathing facilities had not been installed, presumably because of the beginning of the war.

Even without the bathtub we felt that our living quarters were decidedly better. None of our windows faced the west wind directly. There was no further need to hang blankets on the window to stop cold air from blowing in. If you wanted hot water you had to fill a pot and boil it. So what! Compared to the DP camps in Hochfeld, Hanau, and Memmingen we lived in a lordly fashion, indeed.

By mid-evening, long after sundown, the move was complete. I started a fire in the bedroom wood-burning stove. The place became pleasantly warm and cozy. I was so tired by this time that I was ready to flop anywhere. Father decided that Grandfather and I would sleep in the kitchen while he, Mother, and newborn Maria took the bedroom. I think I was asleep as soon as my head touched the pillow. It had been a long, long, exhausting day.

The next morning I was awestruck by the view south out of the bedroom window. There were the Alps in all their white winter glory. Right out of our bedroom window! The highest visible peak turned out to be Zugspitze, Germany's highest mountain.

During our stay in this apartment, it was nice to observe the mountain as the seasons changed. In high summer only the highest peaks were white. As autumn approached the snow seemed to descend the mountainsides. When it rained in late September in Augsburg, it snowed on the lower slopes of the mountains. You could almost tell the seasons by the appearance of the Alps.

A few days later, Mother and my new sister arrived from the maternity hospital. Life changed somewhat, but not that much for me. Grandfather found some former Lithuanian jurists with whom he spent a lot of time. Father talked about getting a job with the labor companies. These were paramilitary units composed of DP's. They were situated mostly in the vicinity of Frankfurt Airport. At this point labor companies were merely a conversation topic.

We kids were very rapidly developing street-smarts and started our venture into capitalism. The black market, that is. At this point our scope was benign. We bought vegetables from German farmers and sold them for a considerable profit at the camp.

Adults purchased cows, brought them into the camp, slaughtered them, and sold fresh meat in one basement or another. This was highly illegal, according to the regulations of those days. The German police were totally impotent as they had no authority within the DP camp, so they reported the whole enterprise to the American MP's. As in any illegal situation, one always had stool pigeons. Haunstetten was no exception.

One or two jeeploads of MP's showed up one time and busted a bunch of guys while they were butchering a cow. No one went to jail. The culprits were fined and released. Fines were in Reichsmarks. And all of us were literally loaded, even us kids. Thus fines were paid, experience was gained, and fresh beef continued to be available on a regular basis.

One day MP sirens were heard in the distance before the cow was slaughtered! After the Americans arrived, they searched several buildings with no success despite having reliable information that the animal was in the camp.

After much searching and questioning passers-by, they called over a man they knew from a previous encounter. "I will not arrest you if you tell me where you hid the animal," said the MP sergeant in charge of the detail. The man was reluctant to open up. The NCO threatened to turn the entire camp inside out until he completed his mission. Finally, after repeated assurances by the sergeant, the guy said, "In the attic". The American broke up laughing, got into a jeep, and departed.

How did the cow end up in the attic? Well, one of our gang explained to me that as a kid in Lithuania he was taught, while herding cows, that the proper twisting of a cow's tail will make it walk on a tight-wire, let alone up several flights of stairs to an attic. Necessity is truly the mother of invention.

It was obvious the Americans never really took the beef black market seriously. Penicillin, or a vial of water labeled Penicillin, was the big item. Cows in the attic had no priority at all.

To my great surprise, in late spring of 1947 I was chosen to be a member of the Lithuanian contingent at the 1947 International Boy Scout Jamboree in France. To this day I do not know the exact reason for my selection. Both Mother and Father were pleasantly surprised. Mother was somewhat reserved about sending a thirteen year old on such an adventure. Father, however, was very enthusiastic. "Just think of the experience and education this travel will give him," he said. In the end they both agreed to let me go.

At this point, Grandfather was in the hospital because of "lung congestion". From today's vantage point it is clear that lung cancer was beginning to declare itself. All those years of incinerating and inhaling various herbs and tobacco! Nevertheless, he was discharged. To this day I don't know if the family knew that his days were numbered.

Spring became summer, and preparation for departure to the Jamboree began in earnest. Two other local scouts had been selected. Their names were

Albinas and Algimantas, who was always called by his nickname, Algis. On an assigned day we met at the Augsburg Hbf (Hauptbahnhof) and took a train to Frankfurt. From there we went to Hanau.

On my arrival at the Hanau DP camp, I was astounded to see what a real DP camp looked like. It was housed in a former kaserne, a permanent German army barracks. The buildings were divided into huge halls. Each at one time housed a hundred or more soldiers. The hallways still had racks to hold rifles. Of course, they were now completely empty. Each hall was divided by hanging blankets into areas for one family. That was it. There were no other provisions for privacy. If a baby was crying in one area, the whole hall was kept up. If a man and his wife were having an argument, the rest of the inhabitants were the audience. The bathrooms were barrack style. They were not unisex, however. Inhabitants were fed in huge military mess halls. Unlike in Haunstetten, one couldn't bring the groceries home and cook whatever dish the products allowed or one desired on a particular day. In the mess hall of Hanau, whatever food was dished out was what you ate. Feeding times were posted and strictly adhered to.

We inquired about the Jamboree preparatory camp. Nobody seemed to know what the hell we were talking about. Then one of the men told us there was a Lithuanian scout camp in the vicinity of a neighboring town. One of the locals got hold of a camp truck and gave us Augsburgers a ride. When we got there, we found out that they didn't even know that there was an international Jamboree, let alone a prep camp.

By now it was late morning. We felt tired, skuzzy, and hungry. Our journey was almost entering its second day. Then there was a breakthrough! One scout master knew of the Jamboree and where the preparatory camp was. It turned out that it was within walking distance of the Hanau DP establishment! The guy with the truck, fortunately, was still around. On his way home he was kind enough to drop us off at our final destination.

When our intrepid group arrived, it was assigned a tent. Then we sat down with the rest of the campers for supper. "Showers" was a nearby lake. After sundown there was a bonfire. The usual camp songs made up the greater part of the program. Before these proceedings were over, a senior scout master welcomed everyone and explained the purpose and nature of this encampment. The next day would begin with instruction in military type marching, the selection of a chorus, and lessons in singing the Marseillaise, in addition to the teaching of important scout skills.

After this we went to bed. Tents were round and had ample room for the six of us that made up the Augsburg contingent. Cots and sleeping bags were already there, previously obtained from the American army quartermaster. That night none of us were chosen for guard duty, and very soon everyone was sound asleep.

The next morning, after breakfast, one of the scout masters informed our group of a frightening possibility. We might not all be going to France! However, if the necessary funds were granted by the American Lithuanian Council, then everyone would get to go. Otherwise, ten of us would have to go home. In that case, selection would be made on merit. Whatever that meant.

Camp life gave us no free time at all. From early morning until supper we either marched or sang or worked in camp home keeping. The weather remained good. Every day was sunny and warm, but not too hot. Nights were also comfortable. I had a brief spell of homesickness which soon disappeared because there was no time to sit and brood. The discipline was hard, but we soon got used to it. We generally liked this tightly organized camping.

Preparation was supposed to last two weeks. After some ten days of this, it still wasn't clear if all of us would get to go. One of the scouts, a local from Hanau, somehow concluded that we would all not be able to go to the Jamboree and left camp. Two days later we got good news: everyone could go! Alas, the poor pessimist from Hanau was not readmitted.

Late afternoon of the fourteenth day, several trucks that belonged to the International Refugee Organization picked us up, and we set off for the Frankfurt Hbf, the main railroad station. As our small convoy approached the environs of the station, every one of us became totally silent. None of us had ever seen such total destruction of a city by systematic bombing. There were only ruins and bulldozed streets. We saw no upright remains. There were no walls or chimneys, only mountains of bricks and broken concrete. The scouts in this group had experienced raids in many German cities. There was even one survivor of the Dresden raid. But none of us had seen such removal of a city from the face of the earth.

There were no sidewalks. Pedestrians carrying their bags or fishnet-like grocery containers had to be skillful in dodging traffic. Traffic around Frankfurt Hbf was mainly military. There were few civilian trucks and no civilian cars at all. Many years later, I found out that Frankfurt had been one of the largest railroad centers in the world, second only to Chicago. It paid a terrible price for this fame.

The Jamboree travelers were unloaded by the passenger entrance. The scoutmasters went in to obtain tickets. They had had the necessary travel documents and French visas for some time now.

After a wait of about a half hour, our uniformed group proceeded to the track where the Frankfurt-Paris express was taking on passengers. We attracted considerable attention. The last time the locals had seen kids in any kind of uniform it was the Hitler Jugend. An old lady asked one of us, "Who are these foreigners in these unusual outfits?" She was told, "Litauische Pfadfinder." From her expression I could tell she didn't have the vaguest idea of what "Litauische Pfadfinder" meant. Actually, it was German for "Lithuanian scouts". Germany was so full of various foreigners that her puzzlement was fully understandable.

On the way to the tracks, the absence of the usual station kiosks was very noticeable. There were no food stands, no tobacconists, and no bars - not even news stands. A lonely Red Cross flag indicated the location of a medical aid station. Teams of American MPs accompanied by German policemen were standing in various locations. A German cop checked tickets and other documents at every entrance to the tracks.

Upon boarding we were immediately separated into small groups and spread throughout the entire train. I wound up with two others in a compartment occupied by French speaking civilians. The train pulled out right about sunset and traveled for a good 45 minutes through what was left of Frankfurt.

I don't remember anything about sleeping. I do remember that late the next morning I became very hungry. The French speakers left the compartment and went to the adjoining car, which was the dining car. For me the dining car was out of the question for a simple reason; I had no money. The only food that I had was some white bread. However, I did not wish to appear odd eating just bread. So I took two pieces, put them together, and made like I was eating a sandwich. It really did not look like a sandwich, but by that time I was so hungry I no longer cared.

The train moved through the French countryside at a good clip. Some of the stations I remembered from my study of maps. One particular station stuck in my mind forever. It was Bar le Duc. I never found out what it meant. Years later, while traveling from Basel to Paris, I again passed through Bar le Duc. Again I made a mental note to get an explanation. As of this writing, however, even after speaking with many Frenchmen and French speaking Swiss, I still don't know what Bar le Duc means.

In mid-afternoon the express pulled in to Gare del' Est. We all were impressed with the size of Paris. It took some time for the train just to go through the suburbs to the station. Unlike Frankfurt, Paris had no ruins or other evidence of bombing.

Castle of Kaunas

Sunday morning, Liberty Boulevard, Kaunas, 2003

Typical Prewar Farm House, Central Lithuania

Kaunas, Confluence of Nemunas and Neris

View towards Zeimiai from the Hill of Sirviai, 1992

Palanga, Museum of Amber

Palanga, granddaughter Jordan gathering amber, 2003

Palanga, sea pier

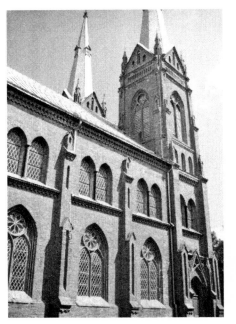

Church at Zeimiai

Roadside shrine, churchyard Zeimiai

Helaine and I at the Hill of Crosses, 1992

Father, 1944

Grandfather Boreisa, 1938

Mother, 1972

Grandfather and Grandmother Olga in their farmer mode, 1930

Gas generator truck. I am on the right with the cap, 1944

Der Reichsstatthalter in Wien

Bescheinigung zur Benützung der Eisenbahn

Herr - Frau - Fräulein ...Gauzinkas... Petras... p. Frau, Kind u.
wohnhaft ..Wien - Neidörfl. Bf. v. Neustadt.............. Webriegerate
                    (Ort,Straße,Hausnummer)
ist berechtigt,
in der Zeit vom ...30.9...... bis ......7.10.1944....
von .....Wien............... nach ...vorgl. (Ort.)...
und zurück zu reisen.
+) 1) Die Reise soll im Auftrage der ....
                              (Behörde,Parteistelle,Firma)
      durchgeführt werden und dient kriegswichtigen Zwecken.
+) 2) Reisegrund ....Arbeitseinsatz............................
      ....

                                    Wien., den 30.9.1944.
                                    ....J.A. Brux..........

Diese Bescheinigung berechtigt zum Lösen von Fahrkarten nur für die
angegebene Reise und gilt nur in Verbindung mit einem Lichtbildausweis.
Sie ist auf Verlangen jederzeit vorzuzeigen.
Jeder Mißbrauch wird strafrechtlich verfolgt.
+) Nur 1) oder 2) ausfüllen und Nichtzutreffendes durchstreichen.

Permission to use the railroad, 1944

Father's provisional German foreigner
passport, 1944

Cameo purchased by Mother after air raid in Innsbruck, 1945

France, Jamboree, 1947. I am in the middle.

Augsburg, with DP friends, 1948. I am in the front middle.

Arrival in Buffalo, July 4, 1949

High School photograph, 1950

After the train stopped, one of our guys got out of it war-fashion like. He opened the window and jumped out. This attracted considerable attention and even greater wrath of one of the scout masters standing nearby. We walked away from the train and, to our surprise, found out that the French expected a person to hang on to the ticket. At the exit an officious-looking individual stopped all who did not have the ticket. I had mine, and so I was allowed to proceed through the gate, into the City of Lights. The scout masters got all those without tickets through the gates after an explanation to the ticket taker. It was good to know that one of the scout masters studied at Grenoble and was fluent in French.

At the sidewalk waited specially designated buses that transported international arrivals to a large dormitory. There we had dinner. The food was OK. Dinner was interesting in that we got salad after everything else was eaten.

At the dormitory, I met a French scout who spoke Russian. This foreign language was my strongest because of Grandmother Olga. The French scout, a grandson of Russian émigrés, was born in Paris. He was essentially a native Parisian.

The next morning, after a good night's rest, the group was driven to the Jamboree located just a short distance from Paris. At the gates to the camp complex, we were directed to an area called Algerie. The entire Jamboree was divided into areas named after French provinces. After falling in, military style, our group set off for Algerie where the Lithuanian contingent from the British and French zones of occupation was already encamped. Our orderly march, accompanied by a marching song, drew favorable attention from many visitors and other scouts.

Finally, we arrived at the gates with the name "Lituanie". We had arrived! Those inside the camp shouted, "Amerikonai atvaziavo!" (The Americans have arrived!). Our column came to a halt. The command to fall out was given, and our next job was to situate ourselves. Which tent? Who will be sharing that tent? Where and when was chow? After we were all settled down, the usual do and don't lecture was given.

That first day we did not wander out of our own compound. The next day, however, we explored the camp. As we walked through other areas, Algerie, Provance, and so on, we found scouts from all over the world. Some of their uniforms were obviously professionally made, if not custom tailored. They had none of the stuff that our uniforms had. None of the individually embroidered scout insignias or merit badges that our uniforms were redundant with.

We noticed American Boy Scouts. They were truly pampered and rather stuck up. Well, they came from a country that, in the short term, had won the war. A country which placed its president among the saints as savior of the western world! A country completely oblivious of the fact that some of the contingents here represented countries which the American president had turned over to Stalin at Yalta.

It was at this jamboree that my political views and experiences began to form my Weltanschaung. This was just one of the factors influencing my character that developed with age, education, and life's experiences and observations. Westerners untouched by war had no real knowledge to grasp what actually happened. This observation was further proven correct when I later arrived in Buffalo and talked, in very limited English, to neighborhood boys. Their knowledge of recent history was so astoundingly limited! None of them knew anything of Yalta. Unfortunately, some of them later paid the price by dying in Korea. Only then did their parents start thinking *maybe the Russians were not our allies!* As of this writing, unfortunately, I still consider our national geopolitical evaluation encumbered by limited awareness.

As we walked through the huge encampment, we met scouts of many nationalities. Using one language or another we sometimes managed to exchange badges and other trinkets. Father had given me two one dollar bills.

At that time the US dollar was worth 212 French francs. I had also been given a few articles of Lithuanian folk art. These were displayed in an ethnic artifacts tent. Each had an affixed price tag. One evening I was told a man was very interested in one of my pieces. I asked a scoutmaster to translate to him that I also had American dollars for sale, but only with the purchase of the wood carving. The guy's eyes lit up. "225 francs," he offered. I started shuffling and told him that Father had said to take no less than 250 francs. Eventually, he said OK. Father had said no such thing, of course, because he had no idea how much a buck was worth in franks. Well, I made a few francs, and I also got my first street lesson; there was such a thing as an asked and an offered price. Where the deal was closed depended on who was smoother.

The next day, our Augsburg group walked all the way to the bank of the river Seine. There was an unwritten custom with our gang that one must swim across any river or lake that one came to. We put on our swimming trunks and started for the other shore.

The Seine below Paris is reminiscent of the lower Mississippi. Crooked like a pigs tail. Without any thought for what could be around the next bend, we reached the middle of the river. We were quite satisfied with our progress. But then the kid who was tail end Charlie started to yell. At first we thought he had a cramp or some other swimming problem, but then he started pointing upstream. The whole group looked to the bend in the river. A beautiful steamer was moving downstream, right about mid-river. Exactly where we were located.

Everyone shifted into high gear and swam for dear life. The whistle on the steamer was not for the benefit of the passengers. It was for us to get the hell out of the way. The entire steamer had now negotiated the bend of the river, and its bow was heading for us. If there was ever a situation where I gave my all, this was it. This was not for a trophy in Muehlbach back in Augsburg; this was to save my ass.

The steamer actually missed us by about thirty yards. We swam to the shore on the opposite side and, exhausted, got out of the water. Panting like dogs on a hot day, the group climbed up the embankment and flopped down on the grass.

At this point I noticed a stream of barges being pushed upstream. The steamer and the barge tug exchanged port-to-port whistles and continued on their way. Well, that was very orderly and nice. How many moving steamers and barges would we have to dodge to get across the Seine and back to the Jamboree? As we sat on the far bank, the traffic on the river did not diminish. We had a discussion. Some argued that we should swim, come hell or high water. Others were not all that enthusiastic. Finally, it was decided that we would all swim together until we reached the middle of the channel. At that point, the fastest swimmer among us, barring the sight of any river craft, would cross the traffic channel and signal from the far side for us to either swim for all we were worth or to tread water. Well, good fortune shone on us. He crossed the mid-channel and started signaling for us to get moving. Even though there were no steamers or barges, we swam like the devil himself was swimming after us.

We made the Jamboree side of the river without anything worse happening than having the hell scared out of us. As we sat and changed into our uniforms, one scout remarked that even though our tradition to cross a body of water had always been uneventful, we had never swum across a navigable river or lake before. That was something to think about. When we arrived in camp, we slowly walked back to the area called "Algerie" and then to the gate labeled "Lituanie". Others asked us about where we had been. We merely answered, "The other side of the river." After they found out that we swam, many concluded that we were intellectually impaired.

The next day was a sightseeing day. A series of buses took us into Paris to appreciate and compare various architectural examples. The first stop was

Notre Dame. In Augsburg our art classes had frequently consisted of actually going to and seeing the architecture we had discussed in class. Although most of us had already seen quite a few examples of gothic architecture in Germany, none of us had ever seen such an indescribably magnificent cathedral.

We climbed the left tower. There the vandal in me asserted himself. I could not resist scratching my initials on the exit turret, which was already covered with scratched graffiti of various vintages. I thought that my initials would remain visible for ever. Such unjustified hubris! When I saw the same turret in 1971, evidence of my vandalism was nowhere to be found. I think that weather and other graffiti erased all trace of my previous visit. *Sic transit gloria mundis.* Thus passes the glory of the world.

After Notre Dame to the Eiffel Tower. Everyone knew of the tower, but no one had the money for the ride to the top. One of the scouts soon discovered that reaching the promenade level was free. Free, that is, if one used the stairs. We figured that looking out at the city from halfway up would be better than just looking at the tower from the ground up. So all of us got up there and enjoyed the panorama of the City of Lights. If there had been stairs to the top, I have no doubt we all would have seen Paris the way I saw it twenty-three years later.

After that, a visit to the Invalides and Napoleon's tomb. Then we went to the Louvre. While I recognized a few statues, my general knowledge of art had not even reached a seminal stage. This was evident by my great interest in paintings of naked women while I ignored the painting of one woman that had attracted a small crowd. Only later did I learn that the solitary painting was La Giaconda, better known as Mona Lisa. Twenty-three years later I stood with Helaine in front of Leonardo's masterpiece and still wondered what all the fuss was about,

After visiting the Louvre, back on the buses and proceed to Versailles. Our first stop there was at the famed palace. We started our tour with a walk through the gardens. They made Schoenbrunn gardens seem somewhat anemic. The sheer size of the park and the fountains left a lasting impression.

After that, into the palace itself. We knew about the eponymous treaty and saw the table on which it was actually signed. The Hall of Mirrors I had only heard about. I hadn't even seen a picture of it. Even at the age of thirteen, it was beyond all my imagination. I felt I was walking through history itself.

On our return to Paris, the buses took us to Montmartre where a most upsetting incident occurred. I got separated from the group and darn near got lost. It was not entirely my fault. An old lady asked me something in French. Although I now have variable fluency in six languages, French wasn't, isn't, and never will be one of them. Nonetheless, I tried to be polite. I pointed to my scout insignia and an inscription on the uniform that read "Lituanie". She then said something else. At the same time I noticed that I could see none of the group. I left the curious woman and ran to the next corner. The group was not in sight. Then I saw people descending stairs from the sidewalk into what was labeled Metro. I ran to the stairs, looked down, and saw the last of our group turning the corner. Within seconds I was back with them. I made a mental note to never again let the other's walk away, even if it required a breach of etiquette.

The next morning, back in camp, I woke up itching all over. Many of the itchy spots had formed papules. To the consternation of the scout masters, it was noticed that this pruritic epidemic afflicted not just me, but a number of scouts and scout masters. No medications, creams, or lotions were prescribed. We were simply told that once we left, this plague would clear up. I had no idea as to the cause of this outbreak. Each papule resembled a flea bite, so I felt it was some kind of bug that was biting us.

Bug or no bug, the next day was the visit of Auriol, president of the Fourth Republic. At that time the longevity of French governments would sometimes be no more than several days. Such was their system then.

We set out to the center of the Jamboree to see the dignitaries. Auriol, thick horn-rimmed glasses and all, was accompanied by general DeLattre deTessigny. The general was their chief of staff or some such person. His name became better known after the French debacle in what was then called French Indochina. He wore a kepi, of course, with more embroidery than MacArthur's field marshal's hat. All in all, seeing these men was very interesting, even if they were chieftains recently resurrected out of the ruins of defeated France.

The jamboree was coming to a close. Closing ceremonies were held in the central area. Lord Wilson was now the World's Chief Scout. Baden-Powell, the founder of the scout movement, had died some years ago. He was buried where he had lived, at Nyeri, Kenya. Little did I know then that I would visit his grave with Helaine forty-two years later. The ceremonies were replete with speeches in many languages. I did not understand them and couldn't wait for the whole show to be over.

Eventually, the ceremonies ended, and work on cleaning our area began. When we were done, the only thing we left were our footprints.

The next day we boarded the buses. They took us to Gare del'Est, and we got on the Frankfurt express. On the train the digestion of recent events was pre-eminent in our thoughts, although most of us were also thinking of the homes we had left almost one month before. At Frankfurt the group transferred to the Alpen-Nordsee express and sped off to Augsburg. Eventually, I arrived at Flachsstrasse 32.

Mother was home, and her first words were not, "Hello, welcome home, how was the jamboree?" They were, "Have you been told about Uncle Victor?"

While I was away, Uncle Victor came down with acute appendicitis. He was admitted at the local town hospital, and an appendectomy was performed. Aunt Bernice, an experienced nurse, saw that he had been overanesthetized and was afraid of him getting pneumonia. Her fear was not groundless. He came down with pneumonia and died. He had already been buried at the old Haunstetten cemetery by the time I reached home. Aunt Bernice and Jolanta were alone. Alone, far from home, and in a foreign land.

Relatives in Lithuania could not be notified right away. The Red Holocaust was raging full blast at home, and any letters reached their addresses at the discretion of an NKGB censor. Such a letter placed the addressee on the NKGB undesirables list and in jeopardy.

The year 1947 was not a good one in the Gamziukas family. In the fall, Grandfather went back to the hospital. This time things took a long time. Eventually, one rainy and windy autumn day, Mother took me to a place called Servatius Stift. This was a hospital that serviced the DP population of Augsburg. The medical staff consisted of DP physicians.

Now, many years later, I wonder about this fruit salad of training, experience, competence, and dedication. How were these doctors credentialed? How were their privileges granted? The reader will understand the problems we faced if he is informed of the methodology of the average American hospital.

A graduate of an American medical school does a one year internship in general medicine. He or she then proceeds to a specialty residency which may last from three years, for a primary field such as general internal medicine, all the way to seven years for neurosurgery. When a physician applies to a hospital for permission to practice, he supplies all documentation concerning his training and experience. This is carefully examined and verified by a credentials committee. If the recommendation is positive, a series of questions follow. What privileges can the physician be given? What can he actually do at the institution? Can he operate without supervision? Can he treat the gravely sick, or only those that do not require someone trained in intensive care? While it is understandable that in the forties even American medicine did not have such an elaborate methodology of acceptance, this system is effective in ensuring quality health care.

At that time, I had no idea who was Grandfather's attending physician or what his qualifications were. I also didn't know anything about the other personnel who were treating him. By today's standards of peer review, it was a shot in the dark whether or not my Grandfather received quality care.

On an appointed day, Mother brought me to see him. I had never been so shocked in my life. The entire scene was that of horror. In the bed was a living human skeleton attempting to say something and reaching for me. I couldn't believe this was my Grandfather. His appearance was like the concentration camp prisoners in the documentary film called "Todesmuhle" (The Mill of Death). I could not understand what he was trying to say, and though he was reaching for me I just wanted to get out of there, to leave this private death chamber.

At that age I had not seen any real illness. In the declining days of my Grandmother Boreisa's life, I had somehow been kept away. It seems the last time I had seen her alive she was ambulating. She certainly had not been a skeleton like Grandfather was now.

Finally, Mother allowed me to wait in the corridor. I found the door to a patio and walked outside, where the air was fresh and the stench of death did not add to the fear and depression of the living. I wanted to get away from the hospital, the doctors, and the nurses. I recall very vividly that I wanted to be in the woods, away from sickness and the intense sadness that it brings to all. A few hours later, Grandfather Boreisa, Justice of the Supreme Tribunal of the Republic of Lithuania, died.

Grandfather was first laid out in the hospital chapel. Then he was transferred to the little chapel of the Haunstetten old cemetery. From there he was buried. At the gravesite there were eulogies by senior jurists who had managed to escape to the West. I don't recall at all what they were saying.

Perhaps I was not listening, remembering instead the happy times I had spent with Grandfather riding horses in Sirviai or walking along the streets of Vienna where he told me many historical facts about the city. He had been a wealth of information to an interested boy. In Augsburg he had taught me the history of the city and the significance of the religious wars of the Reformation. I learned that Hitler had only once visited the city in his glory days. Grandfather also told me that he would rather sleep on the hardest rock in Sirviai than in the softest bed outside of his country. And now he was gone. Gone like Uncle Victor a few months before. When I returned to our apartment and saw his empty bed, I was overwhelmed by profound sorrow. I cried and cried until Father entered. He took me by the shoulder and said, "Remember, he is in a place which has no wars, no Bolsheviks, and no tears."

Mother sent the sad news to Grandfather's brother Joseph in Buffalo. Although the 2003 telephone directory of Kaunas listed some fourteen Boreisas, none of them appeared related.

Life in camp continued as usual. School was going well. Although I was a hell raiser, my grades were unassailable.

Our black market activities in Köenigsplatz were becoming more and more sophisticated. We were now selling American cigarettes one or two at a time. This, of course, was done at a considerably better mark up than full packs. The selling of the previous day's movie tickets to people in a queue had mixed results, however. Quite a few were too smart for such low tricks. However, as an American street-smart circus man said, "A sucker is born every minute." We also bought apples from farmers and sold them at a camp for considerable profit. This was lucrative, but highly seasonal.

The most profitable of all our schemes was our seminal cancer prevention program. It was simplicity itself. We discovered that empty, discarded packages of American cigarettes were ubiquitous. They could be found in gutters, sidewalks and mesh trash cans attached to light posts. To an enterprising mind they were not trash, not by a long shot. It was further discovered that corrugated paper had almost the same weight as cigarettes. The minimal weight difference could not be discovered by mere handling, especially on a poorly lit street corner. We realized that our efforts would cut down on smoking and enhance the health of the purchaser, but would endanger our own health if we were discovered. Therefore, it was decided that this would be a high volume, one time promotion.

Even in those young days, our marketing sense was almost as good as that of big corporations on the other side of the Atlantic. We started a highly structured enterprise. This was not every one for himself; this was an organizational effort. Today, American corporations are in love with the words "team effort". Well, I suppose this was a primordial "team effort."

First, we prepared the merchandise. Corrugated paper was cut, and the discarded packs were filled and resealed. The product was divided among the four of us, and various "market" areas were determined. The decision was made to run the sale for just one day in key black market areas of the city. No effort was spent on advertising. We would saturate the market once and only once. To continue the operation after that would be dangerous.

Revenues from this cancer prevention effort were beyond all our expectations. With just a slight price reduction below the usual street value, we sold out our entire stock.

During the next few days, we realized that there was a price to pay. A price on which a monetary amount could not be placed. No one talked of it, but everyone in our group felt that we had done something very wrong. Everyone had a conscience and was feeling the pangs of moral pain. Though we had been dealing in places known for black market activity, the majority of people there were not crooked. If some poor nicotine addict had been trying to satisfy his craving, then we had taken advantage of him. I felt that I had sinned against God and my fellow human. Well, I must admit this was morally the darkest episode in my life. It was not some sermon or lecture, but an epiphany. This despicable undertaking showed me it is never worth doing wrong to get money.

We never talked about this abominable affair. No one ever again suggested any shady method for making an extra Reichsmark. Looking back from the perspective of many years in the future, I am gratified to know that all of us grew up to be solid citizens in our communities and our chosen fields of endeavor.

In the winter of 1947/48, I went through a lot of changes as a result of growing up. Childish interests were gradually being replaced by a more mature attitude on matters and issues before me. Father started work in Giesen as the pay master for a Lithuanian labor corps. He came home for most weekends. His camera, a superb Leica 3B, was always at home. Although I never asked permission, I became a fledgling photographer and started using his camera. Some of the pictures are still in my possession. A direct, un-enlarged print of a negative was all that was available in the camp. Today's computers, however, helped a lot in making these old pictures viewable. They are very interesting as they represent life in Haunstetten DP camp.

Right about this time, a deeper interest in current events began showing itself in various questions and doubts in my mind. We were in Germany because the Bolsheviks were in Lithuania, and yet the western press was trying to tell me that Europe had been liberated with the elimination of Hitler. Some retrospective articles used the term "liberated by the Red Army". Something was wrong with this term.

At about this time, Russian officers began appearing in DP camps. The purpose behind these visits was to get DP's to return to their home countries. The officers would target specific people, ask for interviews, and hope they could get the subjects to return home. The Soviet officer would always be accompanied by two MP's in an American military police jeep. Presumably, the

Americans were there to ensure that the Russian did not engage in any overly forceful tactics. In reality, the Americans were totally oblivious of the Russian's activities. Most of the time they flirted with attractive girls who passed by. These females were the focus of their attention. They also did not give a damn about the Russian vehicle. This was not lost on our gang.

During one of the Russian visits, one of the older boys in our group figured out that if something rolled off of the two-story roof it would land on the Russian's car. So, as an experiment, a small stone was thrown on the roof. It rolled down and, to our delight, landed on the hood of the target car. However, it hardly left a mark. The ballistics were established, but we needed improvement to inflict some damage. We threw larger stones on the roof, but again the effect was only chipped paint, not even a dent in the metal of the car.

At this point we realized that the MPs had noticed what we were up to. We got ready to get the hell out of there if they reacted. Fortunately for us, and lamentably unfortunate for the Russian car, the Americans' interest returned to two stunning Estonian blondes. The green light was on! But we had to come up with a more effective method.

One of our crowd, a guy named Jonas, came up with the solution. He went in the building. A few moments later he stuck his head out of the attic vent. This was essentially a hinged window in the roof. Jonas disappeared, and then reappeared with a clay roofing tile. He carefully placed it on the steeply slanted roof and gave it a shove downward. The tile tobogganed down, flew through the air, and landed squarely in the middle of the car's windshield! The impact was considerable. The entire windshield was one big broken glass star. By that time the roof vent was already closed, and Jonas was standing behind our group. Just another innocent spectator.

The Americans stopped their conversation with the blondes. *Now all hell will break out*, I thought, and got ready to run. However, an older boy behind me ordered everyone to stay put. "Otherwise," he said, "the MPs will think we had something to do with it." So our group of angels stood there and watched the Russian major come out of the building. He examined the windshield. Then, without even saying anything to the MPs, he dropped his cigarette butt, got in the car, and slowly drove off. The American jeep followed some distance behind.

This, however, was not the worst thing that happened to comrade major. A few weeks later he was waiting at the Augsburg main station, along with many other people, for a train to Munich. As the train entered the station, comrade major was mysteriously propelled onto the track, in front of the onrushing locomotive. What a pity.

One cannot say that Russian efforts to repatriate people from the Baltics were entirely wasted. In Haunstetten, Mrs. Smailiene, a recent widow with a young child, decided to go back. Many of her friends and neighbors tried to talk her out of it. Alas, their efforts did not change her mind. Looking back, I cannot totally disagree with her decision. She had recently lost her husband and had a young child to look after. The future for her, as for all of us, was one big question mark. Maybe to return home was the better choice. After all, she reasoned, it was her husband, Smailys, that the Russians had been after, not her.

Before she left, however, she was clever enough to devise a method of communication that was, in effect, an unbreakable code. She told a close friend that after a few months she would write letters to several of her DP camp friends describing Lithuania under Russian rule and relating her own experiences. She told only her closest friend that if the letters were written in pencil they would describe the truth, and if in ink they would be lies.

Several months went by before the first of four letters arrived. Smailiene was very happy with her decision to return. Conditions, even after the recent war, were not at all bad. Their home was undamaged, and there was enough to eat for all. She gave the impression that life was returning to normal.

The letters were written in black ink.

At the labor company, where Father was now well established, men had privileges of shopping at the PX. One of the first things he did was buy me a brand new pair of American army shoes. I finally returned to wearing shoes that were a matched pair. I no longer had to stand with one foot behind the other; the multitude of cracks about my German army footwear ceased at last. (The shoes I wore to the Jamboree were borrowed for the occasion and had to be given back on my return from France.)

Sometime in early summer, Mother fell down the stairs leading into the basement and broke her left wrist. With Maria being just one year old, I helped Mother with various household chores and the work entailed in the care of my sister. I had to stand in many a queue to bring home rations and milk, and I generally tried to minimize the work for Mother. Father was away in Giessen most of the time and provided the only income we had. He also continued the efforts started by Grandfather on the possibility of our emigration to the USA.

The contact established by Walter Brazer had evolved into a regular correspondence between Grandfather and his brother Joseph in Buffalo N.Y. After Grandfather's death, Mother had picked up where Grandfather had left off. Eventually, this correspondence led to our family receiving an affidavit from Buffalo. This document, which most Displaced Persons were trying to obtain from their relatives in the states, simply stated that the immigrant would not become a receiver of public assistance, and that he would not become any sort of burden on the public. In all such cases, the American relatives went way out on a limb for their refugee kin. The American had to guarantee employment, housing, and medical care. Welfare and entitlements had not yet been invented in the waning days of the first half of the twentieth century. The idea of an American doing nothing and getting paid by the state of New York, however, was in not too distant future.

After all documents had been submitted to the emigration authorities, the family had to wait for "the number". The number was concrete evidence that one had a place in the transportation queue. People discovered their number by the daily checking of a bulletin board where emigration notices were posted. I recall the bulletin board very well. It was a hexagonal wooden structure reminiscent of the round European city advertising post, usually replete with theater, movie, and political posters. The numbers were posted by the nationality of the emigrating DP: Lithuanians on one panel, Latvians on another, etc. A separate panel listed those traveling to countries other than the USA. The scattering of Baltic DPs was truly a global dispersal.

Canada was the second most popular destination. Most of these emigrants went on some sort of a year-long contract. Some went to be lumberjacks, some to be factory workers, and some to be housekeepers. Years later it was amusing to find out that some Canadians had thought Europe was supplying them with domestic servants. These Canadian families had deemed themselves to have "arrived" in the social sense. In most cases, though, the hosts were from the undereducated blue collar class, while their "servants" usually held university degrees.

Other notable destinations were Australia and New Zealand. A smattering went to Argentina, Brazil, Uruguay, or Venezuela. Eventually, after variable lengths of stay in the countries they initially emigrated to, many ended up in America.

The first step prior to leaving the camp was a physical exam. This included a 35 mm chest X-ray and the Wassermann blood test, which was at that time the state of the art serologic analysis of blood for syphilis. Flunking this test meant you weren't going anywhere. No country allowed syphilitics in. Evidence of tuberculosis was equally disqualifying.

There were some shenanigans with the Wassermann test. Blood samples could be switched, for a price. One prominent Lithuanian jurist was found to have positive serology. On repeat analysis, however, his blood was clean. This could only mean that some unknown syphilitic traveled overseas on the negative serology of the respected appeals court judge. Well, no system was perfect.

Those that remained in Germany after the camps closed were in a fix. Some 7000 Lithuanians stayed in Germany for various reasons precluding emigration. The German economy was in ruins, and life must have been very difficult. Some, however, did remarkably well. They became proficient in the language, acquired a university-level education, and became professionals.

After our family got the number, we began packing. Father acquired huge duffel bags to hold all our belongings. By that time I had accumulated a batch of things of my own. Most were various war mementos of no value. One item, however, was something else. It was an intact Nazi eagle holding a swastika.

Once, back in 1945, I watched a railroad workman knocking Nazi emblems off of rolling stock in a nearby marshalling yard. As he moved along the side-tracked train, I made off with the aluminum emblem. It was an eagle, completely undamaged, with a wing spread of some eighteen inches. No damage was even caused by its unceremonious removal from the railway carriage.

To a twelve-year old not too well versed in Nazism it represented only a beautiful emblem. I had kept it hidden for three years among my things, and no one in the family knew of its existence. However, Father noticed it while the family was packing for the journey. All hell broke lose. Where did I get it? What was I doing with it? Was I demented enough to think of bringing it to America? Well, all of the inquiries were answered, and Father told me to get rid of it.

I had no intentions of just throwing it away. I had to hide it somewhere. Somewhere known to me alone. There was an open field some 200 meters away from the camp. At the edge grew an old oak. What a great landmark! I got a beat-up spade and buried the eagle exactly two meters due north of the tree. I measured all distances with a measuring string and the bearing with my scout compass. I even knew I had buried it exactly fifty centimeters below the surface. I felt better. Should I ever return I would know where the bird was. And, who knew, maybe future circumstances would allow me to retrieve this treasured possession.

Some 20 years later I returned to Haunstetten with Helaine and went to see the old DP camp. I came to the edge of the housing development the camp had become. All the time my thoughts were on the bird. Eventually, we found the spot where the old oak had been. Alas, there was no oak! The field was gone also. In its place was a group of seven-story apartment buildings with streets and parking lots in between. Well, the only thought that came to me was this: the new housing project had a Nazi emblem for its foundation.

The family packing continued. We all went to bid farewell to the graves of Uncle Victor and Grandfather Boreisa. Their gravestones described one as lieutenant of the Lithuanian army and the other as a Justice of the Supreme Court of Lithuania. The cemetery, today known as The Old Cemetery, contains a few other gravestones with Lithuanian names. These were people forced out of their homes and country, and who ended up buried in an obscure cemetery in a foreign land.

As the departure day grew nearer, we said our goodbyes to friends and acquaintances. We were not the only departing family. Aunt Bernice and cousin Jolanta were traveling with us as well. While we were heading for Buffalo, a city with no Lithuanian population, they were heading for Chicago, a city with the third largest Lithuanian population in the world.

I attended my last day at the Gymnasium. The school was a shadow of its former self. Many students and teachers had already left for distant destinations. I was promoted to sixth class and given an attestation describing my courses of study and my performance in those studies. All of this took place in early June. I knew that in September I would be attending a school thousands of miles away. I said goodbye to a few classmates whom I had known for four years and with whom I had spent my early teenage years in the ruins of Germany, particularly in Augsburg. We promised to correspond. Most of them were also waiting for emigration. Most went to the USA. However, one wound up in Medellin, Colombia, and another in far away New Zealand. They, as medical jargon goes, were lost to follow-up.

I had a bicycle. It had been purchased for twenty DM (Deutschemark) from another boy one class below me in school. It had been put together out of parts scavenged in various dumps and ruins. It had a pneumatic rear tire, the front wheel had a garden hose for a tire. The bike had a front-wheel driven generator and a powerful light which threw an impressive beam. Mine was the only such bike in the entire DP camp, and the light was the envy of all the other junk-bike owners. It is funny, but today I cannot recall what happened to my bike. I am sure that I did not lean it against the wall somewhere and walk away. Most likely I gave it to some kid who was not in the emigration pipeline at the time of our departure.

Certain vignettes of those days come to memory. For instance, my geography teacher stopped me one afternoon and gave me an impromptu oral exam. "Where is Buffalo?" was his first question. "Between Lake Erie and Ontario," was my answer. "What world famous geographic feature is nearby?" he queried further. "Niagara Falls," I answered. After making some remark about my familiarity with where my family was going, he wished me all the best and continued toward the community building.

It was high summer of 1949, and the weather in this part of Bavaria was very warm, if not hot. On sunny days the Alps were clearly visible out of our window. Zugspitze's pinnacle was covered with snow, as were the tops of the mountain range. The slopes looked green.

Sometime in early June our scout patrol had its last picnic on the beach-like bank of the Lech. We brought a large pot, some potatoes, onions, and few pieces of beef. A loaf of black rye bread was also part of the feast. Everyone had his mess kit with him.

When I look back on this outing, I realize that it was the last of my childhood. Scouting in Augsburg was a great developmental and outdoor skill-building experience. Many years later it paid big dividends on a canoe trip in Algonquin when I was accompanied by my twelve year old son, Paul. Augsburg, scouting, and camping indeed marked the second and last halcyon period of my life. Changes, great changes were just around the corner

Chapter Eight

Quite a number of trucks arrived to take the emigrants to the railroad yards. It was about midmorning, and a number of our family's camp friends came to say farewell. We then boarded the trucks. They pulled out through many waving hands and shouts of goodbye and good luck.

It did not take much time to get to the southern marshaling yards where a train was standing on a siding. It consisted of old passenger carriages. The emigrants, ourselves included, jumped off the trucks and boarded the old train. However, since the departure time turned out to be some time away, we quickly got out again.

As the tracks were very near Hochfeld, quite a few of my Hochfeld school mates were there. Most of them I never saw again. Initially, there was correspondence, but this became less frequent with time and eventually stopped completely. Since I wound up in a city with no Lithuanian population to speak off, I assimilated into the American mainstream much faster than others. The obverse of that was that I lost contact with school friends who moved to live in cities with a large Lithuanian presence and cultural activity.

Even though times were tough immediately after the war, my contemporaries and I had a marvelous time in Augsburg. Memories linger on into advanced age, and I sometimes find that this historic city is closer to my heart than most other cities in Germany, let alone the world.

From Wattens to Augsburg two things had occurred. I had become almost five years older, and my German had become very conversational, if not fluent.

The train was already moving as I bid my last goodbyes and jumped on board. The train proceeded to Munich where we were housed in an old "caserne". The next day we were taken back to the station, boarded a train of considerably later vintage than the previous one, and headed north. This train essentially bisected all of Western Germany into eastern and western halves. It traveled from Munich to Bremerhaven. On arrival, all the passengers were taken to a relatively new complex of army barracks. Here we had our final examination of documents and a health check.

I feel that this checkpoint was similar to Ellis Island in the olden days. In 1949, once a person successfully passed through Bremerhaven he was allowed into the States. In fact I did not know of Ellis Island until about 1952.

While our family was being processed, another fifteen year old and I decided to explore the building in which we were staying. Eventually, we made our way to the roof and into the flak tower, where we were promptly detained by the camp police. The worst of this experience happened when Father came to claim me. He read me the riot act all the way back to where we were staying. The most incisive remark was his disappointment with my intellectual development.

We were in the camp for a number of days. One of these days was very warm, so some other Lithuanians and I went swimming in the river Weser. Maritime traffic was considerable. Because of that, our old dictum "you must swim across it" did not even come into question. There was no beach and no sign concerning swimming. For all we knew, we might have been swimming in raw sewage flowing towards the North Sea.

A few more days went by before a list appeared on the bulletin board. The names on it were of the people who would depart on U.S.N.S General R.L.

Howze the next day. Our name was on it, and we immediately started getting ready.

The next day we boarded a beat-up old train on which we took our last land journey in Europe. The train stopped on the pier where the military transport was moored. Everyone left the train and made for the gangplank where a one-armed Navy officer called the roll. When our name was called, we walked up the gangplank to the ship. Once there, an enlisted man directed Father and me to deck "D"; Maria and Mother were assigned to another part of the vessel. Maria was now a toddler. She hung on to Mother's hand as they moved toward the bow and disappeared from view.

When I arrived at my assigned bunk, I found out there were four bunks in adjoining pairs. They were stacked from floor to ceiling. Since the ship was only half-full, one could be selective. Father took the second from the floor, and I chose the one directly above him.

Having settled in, I went up on deck. There were still quite a few people standing in line at the foot of the gangway. I circled the ship on the upper deck, and then descended to a much narrower passageway that opened to the sea. I suppose on luxury liners these would be called promenade decks. Well, the General Howze was a troop carrier, not a luxury liner.

Something strange happened after the last person got on board. Two sailors brought some luggage from the ship to the gangway. The sailors were followed by two or three other people. One of the sailors told me and two other boys to take the luggage off the ship. Followed by the owners of the suitcases, we deposited the luggage at the foot of the gangplank and quickly got back on board. I had no idea what that was all about. Why were these people thrown off the ship just when it was ready to cast off? Shortly after I got back on, the land workers started casting off the lines. A few minutes later there was discernible movement. The ship started out to sea as the sun neared the horizon.

Most of the passengers were on deck looking back at the receding shore. I am sure many were lost in similar thoughts. Goodbye! Will it be forever? Will I ever see these shores or my homeland again? As a fifteen year old, however, such melancholy thinking was not what kept my mind occupied. To me this was again the beginning of a great adventure. Something totally new and exciting was waiting for me on the other side of the Atlantic Ocean.

After passing Helgoland, on our starboard, I went below to eat supper.

The next evening someone said that the ship was entering Pas de Calais (the English Channel). Father and I went on deck. There, again to starboard, was Dover, lit up like a Christmas tree. Many smokestacks and masts were sticking out of the water, twinkling in the reflection of the lights. These relics of the war now posed a hazard to navigation.

This scene soon faded into the distance, until only an occasional light was visible on shore. "It's late," said Father, and we turned and went below. Once in the bunk, I fell asleep in minutes.

The next day started with a morning shower. That was an experience. The water was warm and felt good. No matter how I tried, though, I could not get lather out of the bar of soap. The salty sea water in the shower just would not cooperate with it. Nonetheless, I felt cleaner after this interesting ablution.

Then it was off to breakfast. The mess hall had no chairs or seats of any kind. The tables were fastened to upright poles and came to the height of lower chest. The edges were flanged to prevent spillage on the floor during rough weather sailing. Nevertheless, they were quite comfortable. The food on board was quite good and plentiful. Caffeine addicts were in heaven. They had all the coffee they could drink. That was true for all meals.

After breakfast, we went up to the deck. There was just water all around; no land was visible. A stiff breeze blew along the deck. There were a few whitecaps, but otherwise the ocean surface had no large waves. I looked over the bow and noticed that the ship had a rhythmical, up and down motion. The bow would rise slowly above the horizon and then, just as slowly, descend below it. As I observed the ship and the sea, a life boat drill was announced over the loudspeaker. Just as I was getting ready to photograph someone upchucking their breakfast into garbage can, Father told me to hurry up and go below.

I arrived at my bunk, donned my life preserver, and was ready to go to my assigned boat station. At this point, despite being several decks below the top deck, a dizzy feeling started to make me feel uncomfortable. I had never experienced this sensation before. A few minutes went by, but there had been no call to go to the boat station.

At this point I was sweating profusely, and my stomach felt like I had eaten something bad. I thought I had to get into fresh air or I would be sick. As soon as the signal was given to go to the boat station, I moved. I reached the garbage can just in time. Profuse emesis got rid of breakfast and, I thought, my previous three meals. Afterwards, I felt better. I noticed others vomiting over the rail. The boat crew directed them to the garbage cans. I suppose they did not want the passengers to dirty the ocean.

After maybe thirty minutes, the horrible feeling came back. Inadvertently, I glanced at the bow as it rose above the horizon. That was enough to empty my stomach again. This course of events continued for almost three days. During that time I did not give a damn if America fell off the edge of the world or if the ship sank. Eventually, this mal de mer began to let up. I was getting my sea legs. My appetite returned. Many others, however, were still under the influence of the ground swells of the ocean. They were not seen in the mess hall.

Mess personnel told us to eat all we wanted. There was chicken, pork chops, and beef, as well as mashed potatoes and vegetables. I was not in the least bashful. I pigged out.

The next day the sky became leaden, the wind freshened, and the ship at times sprayed considerable spindrift. The ocean was covered with whitecaps, and the waves were much higher than they were the previous day. Clearly we were sailing into a minor storm. Another Lithuanian boy and I were standing behind an upward curved bulkhead on the lower walkway. From here we could see the ocean and dodge any larger spindrift. It was an interesting experience, and we were no longer seasick, even with the more pronounced rocking and rolling of the ship.

Every morning a mark representing our position was placed on the chart pinned to the bulletin board. On an average day the ship traveled slightly over 400 nautical miles. I had no idea if that was fast or slow. Years later, I researched the statistics of our transport. It could carry 3500 soldiers, and its maximum speed was eighteen knots. That was not bad. When Helaine and I took a cruise to Alaska in 1988, the ship did nineteen knots.

After many more days, the bulletin board chart indicated that we would arrive in New York the next day. I was already in my bunk when Father told me that shore lights were visible in the distance. We all made for the deck. Even Mother and Maria were there. Off the starboard bow were city lights, as well as the headlights of vehicles on the road paralleling the shore. I overheard a discussion about where we were. Some said this was Brooklyn; others disagreed. I didn't have the foggiest idea where exactly we were. Somewhere off Long Island was close enough for me.

The next morning, the ship was stopped in the Bay, and some officials boarded from a small motorboat. I assume they were customs/immigration and public health officers. In a few minutes, we were underway again. We passed the Statue of Liberty and approached Manhattan.

In all our years in America, Mother never went to see the Statue. She later confided to me that the future had not looked any too happy to her. She was right. Four years later Father died at age 47.

About one hour later, the ship was moored at one of the piers, and the gangway was connected. Our family descended from the ship and reported to the first open customs table. We had nothing to declare. After a cursory search, we were directed to another table labeled N.C.W.C. The letters stood for National Catholic Welfare Council. We all had numbered tags with the previously mentioned letters on them; mine was 97. At this table the officials already had much information about us. They knew we were a family of four on our way to Buffalo, N.Y.

We received instructions in English. Buses were waiting outside; they would take us to Grand Central Station. Railroad tickets were handed to Father, as well as a piece of paper with additional instructions and our time of departure. It was only early afternoon, and we had lots of time to kill. The train was not leaving until 11:30 p.m..

Before going for the buses, we found Aunt Bernice and Jolanta. They were going to Chicago. It seemed all other Lithuanians were going to Chicago! I felt like my immediate family was traveling to a real unknown. While we were on board the ship, I had often been asked about our destination. My answer had evoked various remarks, the most common of which was, "Where the hell is Buffalo?"

We bid Aunt Bernice and Jolanta a tearful good-bye and wished them all the best. We would not see them again for six years. A few minutes later, after all the farewells, we boarded a bus and continued our journey.

Chapter Nine

Manhattan was sweltering in midsummer heat. The next day, the Fourth of July, promised to be even hotter. Men carried their jackets in their arms instead of wearing them. Since it was so hot, I wondered, why were they wearing hats? The bus taking us to Grand Central Station was a real hot box, even with the windows open.

After we arrived at the cavernous edifice, Father and I checked the timetable and settled down in the waiting hall. We had a long wait ahead of us. Maria was so tired that she promptly fell asleep on the bench.

As there were no further organizations looking after us, we had to fend for ourselves. Fortunately, Father had saved up sufficient cash from his job with the labor corps. There was a food/soda counter nearby. Father ate alone. I stayed with Mother and Maria and watched our possessions until he came back. Then it was our turn.

After eating a sandwich and a coke, I stepped from the station onto 42nd street. The multitude of people and vehicles was overwhelming. I decided that it would be wiser to just take a walk and not cross the street. Even though we had many hours of waiting, I did not walk far. I guess uneasiness about strange places kept me near the station. Eventually, the sun set and the city's neon lights took over. I never even imagined that there was a city with so many neon lights. Father, who had traveled through many great European cities, had to admit that he was amazed as well.

It was near our time to board, so we headed for the track. When we arrived at the train, I was impressed by its gleaming coaches, extremely large windows, and that the floor of the train was at the same level as the platform. There were no stairs to climb. A person simply walked from the platform on to the train. And when we finally got on board, all of us immediately noticed how cool and dry the air was. This was heaven compared to the humidity of Manhattan.

The train left on time. It changed from electric to diesel locomotive and accelerated into the night.

The train's technology impressed me to no end. Its sleek and gleaming design, large windows, and air-cooling were all wonders. Its speed, however, was no faster than the electric trains in Germany. Nor was it cleaner than other trains I had been on, except when compared to a European steam local. Nonetheless, it was impressive for a fifteen year old.

I find it unfortunate that fifty-some years later American trains remain essentially the same. It still takes eight hours to travel between Buffalo and New York, just like it did in 1949. What was once superb remained in a time warp. Bullet trains, TGV's, and intercity expresses exist in foreign countries on far-away continents. Our daughter, Lynn, has observed that trains in the US are mostly used by people who don't own a car and have no money to use a plane.

The countryside became visible as morning dawned. Judging by the watch we were three-quarters of the way there. The country around us resembled northern Bavaria. For that matter, it could have been Lithuania. We passed by rolling hills, well-kept farms, and beautifully green fields. Automatically-controlled grade barriers and paved roads were spread throughout. My first impression was that I liked what I saw.

One oddity I noticed was the abundance of tiger lilies. My Grandmother Olga had made a great effort to keep an area of these flowers in her formal English garden, and here they grew wild in ditches!

We stopped briefly in Rochester, and then we went to Batavia. I wondered, "Is this a Dutch area? Batavia is the name of the capital of the Dutch East Indies." Well, a few years later I discovered that the Dutch East Indies were no more. The country was now called Indonesia, and the capital was called Djakarta.

The Dutch getting kicked out was just one small result of the recent war. The Colonial empires were collapsing everywhere, most notably those controlled by the British. India became independent and partitioned into Muslim Pakistan and Hindu India. The British lion had only a few pacific atolls left.

As these thoughts went through my mind, the train was slowing down. We were entering a large marshaling yard. On the left, adjoining the tracks, a row of poplars partially blocked the view. Beyond them was series of wooden two-story houses. At this point the conductor entered and announced our arrival in Buffalo. *Buffalo consists of wooden two-story houses?* The thought seemed horrible to me. Little did I know then that the area was called Sloan, and that the village would be one of the areas I would cover in my medical practice.

The train stopped at the Central Terminal. After making sure that we were not leaving anything behind, we detrained. Maria held Mother's hand as we walked up the stairs to the concourse.

The original convoy which had left Kaunas in the summer of 1944 was at last terminally dispersed. It was the Fourth of July, 1949.

Chapter Ten

O ur family walked through the doors of the terminal and found a small group looking for us. Mother recognized her uncle, Joe Brazer, and we all recognized Walter Brazer from when he visited us in Haunstetten a few years before. We hugged, kissed, and shook hands. This was the culmination of the efforts that started with Walter's visit in Germany.

After leaving the terminal, we proceeded to their cars. I rode with Walter, who drove, Anne Rich, who was my Mother's other cousin, and Anne's husband, Don. Walter's car was a 1948 Desoto. The other car was a four door Ford sedan.

The two cars started on their ways to Paderewski drive. The Desoto was a convertible and, to me, luxury personified. Noting that a hot day was about to begin, I said in English, "It is awful hot." That remark surprised the hell out of them. All of a sudden the air was filled with the exclamation, "He speaks English!" Unfortunately, I was limited to just a very little high school English. Nonetheless, a conversation of sorts began.

When we arrived at 53 Oakmont Avenue, our family could appreciate the extent to which Joe Brazer went to make us comfortable. The house was a typical Buffalo east-side two-family dwelling with an ample basement. Joe had built a room in the basement for my parents and Maria. Next to it he had installed a shower. I have no idea if the city ordinances allowed that, but there it was.

The following Monday, Father went to work for the Buffalo Meter Company. He worked in a brass foundry. It was extreme labor, and he was not used to it. Every evening when he returned home he was shot to hell.

I got to know some of the neighborhood boys that were near my age. They were a friendly bunch. One day we rode bicycles to the Williamsville Glen. I liked the expedition and was impressed that there was a waterfall in the middle of a suburb.

Walter took me to his cousin's home in Wanakah. The house was located on the top of a steep Lake Erie shore. I got to go swimming. It was the warmest water I had ever experienced outside of a bathtub. Of course, the heat wave had not let up since our arrival.

While talking, in my limited English, with the kids on Oakmont, I heard them say things that I found unbelievable. Here we were in the late summer of 1949. The Berlin airlift was already history. Still, the next door neighbor kid said that Russia was America's greatest ally. Further conversation along these lines disclosed that they had absolutely no knowledge of the truth of Communism. To them, Roosevelt and Stalin had saved Europe from Hitler. After several such discussions, I avoided the subject. Any such conversation was like talking to a pig about Michelangelo. The Korean War would later be an eye-opener to many. Unfortunately, for many this awareness came too late.

The school I attended, Kensington H.S., was just around the corner from my house. The building still stands, but the school no longer exists due to its exceptionally poor performance.

I recall my first day very vividly. While I walked toward the school I thought, "Damn, here we go again. Wattens all over again. This time it's not German, it's English." Well, it was true. For the second time in five years I had to adapt to a new school and a new language.

I reported to the administration and laid out consular translations of all my school certificates. There was no question, even to a most casual listener, of my English language limitations. Still, some genius of a councilor sent me upstairs to take an IQ test. I had never even seen a multiple choice exam, and I could barely understand the language it was written in. Therefore, when I took the exam I got a forty-five. Another genius, I will refrain from mentioning her name, told me to come back the next morning. I showed up and took the exam again. This time I got a fifty-something. Apparently, the officials in that highly developed department were unaware that such tests were inappropriate for non-English speakers. As a result, I was accepted as a freshman. I knew that all my peers in Chicago had been accepted as juniors, but I didn't have the English to argue such a complex situation. I had to submit to this most intelligent decision.

I took all the freshman courses. Some subjects I had taken two years before. English, of course, was something new. I read the usual books, and my language skill grew exponentially. At the end of the first semester my GPA was ninety-four. The English teacher gave me some second year books to read in addition to the freshman novels. I was moving on a faster track, but I was still a freshman.

The second semester was also a departure from the usual in that I started taking American history, a third year subject. This was difficult initially, but because of my love of history I found it very interesting. At the end of the second semester my GPA was still in the nineties, where it remained through the entire year.

On the last day of school, I was called to the principal's office and informed that in the fall I would be a junior. That was real nice of him. I knew I would be in the last year of high school while my Augsburg friends in Chicago would be starting college.

The summer of 1950 started with very hot weather. By then my parents had bought a house on James Street in the Fillmore–Clinton area of the city. It was a sweatbox, even with all the windows open. It had been built sometime after the Civil War, most likely as a single home. Apparently, the second flat had been added behind the first, many years after the erection of the original, making it a very long house. We lived in the back, and a Lithuanian family by the name of Grikis lived in the front.

The two flats had one toilet that was located between them. In effect, the toilet area was the passage between the front and back flats. The luxury of a bathtub, however, was only in the front. We bathed strictly according to a previously worked out schedule.

There was no cellar. A small attic was big enough to be used as a storage space for seldom used objects. Initially, the back flat had no hot water. Later, a water tank and heater were installed. Heat in both flats was provided by gas burning space heaters. These were quite sufficient to keep things cozy, even on the coldest winter nights.

Behind this long building was a small yard with a small lawn. A lone peach tree constituted the "orchard". This tree was quite prolific and obviated the need to buy peaches. Father was only earning $42 a week, so every penny counted. Those were the days when one could still buy quite a few things for pennies.

The price paid for this house was $4,500.00. The down payment was made by the Brazers, who also held the deed. My parents made mortgage payments to the Marine Trust Company. The entire transaction was a gentlemen's agreement. At some later agreed time, after the down payment had been paid off to the Brazers, the building would become Gamziukas property for the sum of one dollar.

James Street was a very narrow one-way street. None of the houses had a driveway. Space between the buildings did not exceed five feet from wall to wall.

Only once in the nine years I lived on James Street did I see a snow-plow. Usually, street snow removal was done by every owner shoveling in front of his house. Owners were responsible for the street as well as the sidewalk. Shoveling between the buildings was a real job. There was no room to throw the snow sideways. I would start in the middle and shovel toward the street. Then I would change direction and shovel from the middle toward the backyard.

The entire neighborhood was old and inhabited by lower-middle to the lowest socioeconomic class of people. However, the street was always clean. There was no trash or garbage on the street or sidewalks. All the houses were kept up; no peeling paint or other signs of neglect could be found. Poverty and dirt were certainly not related in our neighborhood.

I discovered that farm labor was available on a daily basis. All I had to do was show up at 4:30 a.m. at the unemployment office downtown and get on any of the trucks that drove workers to the farm. Out in the fields I picked whatever was in season. My first job was picking raspberries; later I picked beans. Work was from sunrise to sunset. The pay was so ridiculously low, two cents a quart for berries and two cents a pound for beans, that only desperate individuals would be found working for a farmer. The most I made in a day was six dollars. I have to note that in those days people had pride that is almost extinct now. It was better to work for pennies than to be on welfare.

About midsummer, Father developed an inguinal hernia. The rupture was repaired at Sisters Hospital by its staff's first formally trained surgeon. During his hospital stay, I visited Father on several occasions. We would talk about things that were of interest to me. He enjoyed answering my questions. This led from a question and answer session to actual discussions of subjects that varied from the production of cigarettes to political events of the thirties.

After he was discharged, Father convalesced at home and watched Maria. This freed Mother to occasionally join me in working on a farm.

Some of the farm days were simultaneously interesting and exasperating. For example, once I got on a truck with a lay preacher. From the time the vehicle pulled away from the curb to the time we returned this man never shut up. His continuous flow of Bible stories was broken only by "praising the Lord." There was audience participation. Everyone yelled "amen" when the preacher's statement required further affirmation. This was a bit of Americana that can only be learned by participating.

In early fall, after school started, I felt I knew enough English to look for a part time job. I answered a help wanted ad looking for a pin setter in a two-lane bowling alley saloon. I applied and got the job. I am sure the job was given to me because I was the first to apply. Any pinhead could set the pins. On the way home, I looked in the paper to see if there was anything better available. Sure enough, a downtown drug store was looking for a clerk.

I did not know if my English was good enough, but I figured at worst they would only say no. So I went for my second job in one day. I guess that was my day. I got the clerk's job. Socially this was higher than setting pins in a saloon and way above picking beans for two cents a pound. My pay would be sixty-nine cents an hour. I was moving up in the world!

I told my new bosses that I would prefer not to handle money. One of them explained what a clerk is expected to do. At that point I either had to go for it or go home. I went for it, and the job became a major turning point in my life. Both of my parents were very happy that the new employers thought I could perform as expected. In any event, it was a clean hands job.

I worked six days a week, from four to seven-thirty on weekdays and eleven to seven-thirty on Saturdays.

The store was located in the financial district. The clientele were mostly office workers of various ranks, from well- known attorneys to elevator operators. Saturday's customers came from a very different socioeconomic stratum. Great lakes seamen, lower Main Street bums, proprietors of various stores, and washed up prostitutes made up just a small sample of the lower Main Street world on Saturday.

Across the street stood the building of Merchant Mutual Insurance Company. My daughter Lisa today works there in the capacity of assistant vice president.

My principal responsibility was to wait on customers. I made milkshakes, sold over-the-counter medications, magazines, cigars, and condoms, and made deliveries. The proprietors opened my eyes to the fact that college education was attainable even if one was a recent immigrant. One of the owners had an affectation that he was an intellectual and a thinker. The other was a low-key, pleasant individual who had no need to create phony images of himself.

At this lower Main Street drugstore, I learned the variegated ways of my new adopted country. I learned American street smarts and began to understand that the school of hard knocks is where one learns the tools for building a successful and respectable life. One comes to understand a new country by mixing and interacting with its people. Living in an immigrant ghetto and clinging to the old ways only hinders one's progress. Nonetheless, I am not suggesting, even in the most remote manner, that one should forget the old ways, one's origins, or one's heritage.

The proprietors were driven, to the detriment of whatever reputation they possessed, by the most unethical avarice. They, indeed, were the original recyclers. When an old pharmacist died, and his store had stood unsold for a year or so, they would offer a nominal amount for all the extant stock. While they acquired some viable items, most were old and outdated by the progress of time and science. These items included half-empty large bottles of cough mixtures, stomach remedies, and bottles upon bottles of hair tonics and antibiotic preparations, which in those days did not have expiration dates. All of this was transported to their Main Street store. New names were created, new labels were typed, and items were broken down into sellable four-ounce bottles. Thus, something that had sat on a shelf in a gallon bottle for many years was given new retail life. Prices were arbitrarily assigned, and I was told to sell these "proprietary remedies".

This sort of underhanded dealing was another part of Americana, a part that I have tried to forget. Unfortunately, the memory is as vivid today as it was fifty-some years ago. There is no way that this foisting of potentially harmful substances on unsuspecting customers could occur today. The original owner is responsible for the disposal of non-usables. He would be just as guilty as the shady operator who made such merchandise available to the ignorant public. Accordingly, this part of Americana does not exist any more . Those that were in this kind of marketing have long since been pushing up daisies.

I graduated from high school in 1952 and started Pharmacy School at the University of Buffalo the following autumn. During my senior year at Kensington, my scholastic performance remained in the nineties.

An announcement was made that preparatory classes would be held for the Regents Scholarship Examination. I showed up for about two sessions. At the third, I was unceremoniously informed that one had to be a US citizen to be eligible to sit for the exam. I had no choice but to get up and leave for the study hall.

After I became a physician, I consulted an attorney concerning the citizenship requirement vis-à-vis the regent's exam. After researching the matter, he told me that somebody had not liked me, and I had allowed that person to get away with kicking me out. There was never such a requirement. Since it was way too late to do anything about it, I let the matter rest. This also became a part of Americana never to be forgotten.

Commencement was held at Kleinhans Music Hall. The program brochure had the usual lists. One of them was "All Honor Rolls". My name was not there. I asked the dyspeptic teacher in charge of the proceedings why my name was not there. "You did not attend this school for four years," he said. Later, I discovered that one individual had made all honor rolls, but had attended the school for only two years. His name was on the "All Honor Rolls" list. Further down the program, still under awards, were the words "German Award Recipient: A. Gamziukas. Not presented at this time". Was it possible that the spirit of bigotry and prejudice had something to do with these events? In summary, Kensington H.S. taught me a lot of negatives about this great country of ours.

Father and I painted 94 James Street during the summer. This beat-up old house looked pretty good when we were done. It was given a white trim and green wall. We also bought some roofing paper and cement and patched where patching was needed. These chores taught me skills for later in life. Most importantly, I realized that house maintenance and other chores can be learned by observing and trying yourself. Formal training is not necessary. The work I am talking about is not rocket science.

Some thirteen years later, Helaine and I built a house. I was smart enough to realize that unless we wanted a cookie-cutter house, I would have to retain an architect. My previous experience made me quite conversant with the architect.

The summer flew by in a wink; most likely because I was anxious to start UB. The University of Buffalo was a private institution founded by Millard Fillmore, who, as is well known, served as President of the United States. When I finished all my studies in 1960, the university was still private, with all of the autonomy that entails. When Maria graduated in 1972, however, it had become part of the State University of New York system and lost all of its independence. Albany had already started ruling it in 1962. Therefore, the institution where I was educated no longer exists. Only the buildings are there.

Starting college may be traumatic for a person who had the luck to spend his life within a familiar two mile radius and be surrounded by his peers.

For example, registration is a daunting process. One has to do it alone without any close guides.

To me, however, this matriculation was neither daunting, nor really challenging. I had been through much more horrendous changes than that of going from high school to college. Orientation was given by junior fellows who, more often than not, were impressed with their own station vis-à-vis the barbarian masses just released from various high schools. Somehow this confused process came to an end, and actual education began.

My English at this juncture was such that no one knew I was a recent immigrant. I spoke fluently and without an accent. I wasn't particularly proud of this accomplishment; I just wondered why most immigrants had an accent, even those who spoke the fluent English of the educated. I found throughout my life that the answer was multifactorial. I will not go into my theory, however, as that is not the purpose of this book.

There were some 125 freshmen in my class. Four years later, only thirty-three got their degree in pharmacy. This is not to say that they all flunked out. Many did, but many others changed their major for reasons other than not being able to hack it. Some students were drafted, and some dropped out for personal reasons. Still, pharmacy school did not have a "peak of difficulty", unlike medical school where it was well-known that if one successfully completed the first and second years of preclinical, one would graduate, barring an exceptional screw-up. Pharmacy school, if anything, got progressively more difficult. In the fifties, the school taught five year's worth of credit hours in four years. That in itself accounted for high attrition rates.

The following is an interesting vignette from freshman botany. The course was not very difficult; the professor, however, was. He was an eccentric, post middle-age bachelor and a martinet who insisted that even a correct answer was incorrect if not presented his way. Some 300 students were in his course. Time came for the midterm exam. The following week, in various recitation classes, the papers were being returned by graduate fellows. They were announcing the professor's terrible disappointment over the results. "However," said one grad fellow, "there were three students who got a perfect grade. All three are in this recitation group." *The sons of bitches*, I thought. *They will move the curve.* The grad student handed me my paper as he passed by my chair. In the right upper corner was a red 100. I darn near choked. At home Father was immensely proud and related a similar event that had happened to him during his university days. A few weeks later, as a reward, he took me to a concert by Leonard Warren. I have never forgotten the baritone aria from "La Traviata" that he rendered in his magnificent voice

When I worked in the drug store, a prominent attorney came in every noon for his lunch milkshake. He apparently took a liking to me. He would spend time in conversation with me, a nobody. He asked me about my college plans and finances. One day he handed me his business card with a man's name and address written on the back of it. This was the man who ran the Buffalo Foundation. The attorney instructed me to call and make an appointment to see him. I did as I was told.

The interview was such, that I could not help but think, I was being tested for general knowledge and my determination to pursue education at UB. After several weeks, I was notified that I had been awarded a $250 scholarship. This amount was one half of my tuition! With the addition of the money I earned in the drugstore, I could continue my education.

School continued, and I maintained a good academic performance. Work downtown, however, was something of a rut. The store was rather anemic in prescription activity compared with my later experience in two other pharmacies. I was not allowed to participate in the filling of prescriptions. I ascribed this exclusion to my still limited exposure in pharmaceutical education. I continued jerking milkshakes and selling cigars, cough syrups, condoms, and tampons. The occasional delivery to a customer's home or office broke up the monotony.

Things went this way until the following summer. The Lithuanian Scout National Jamboree was being held at the Queenston-Niagara on the Lake Park. I made it my business not to miss it. A bus took me to Niagara Falls, New York. I walked across the Rainbow Bridge and hitchhiked to the encampment. Many of my acquaintances from Augsburg were there, so it was a very pleasant weekend. All of my contemporaries were at one university or another. Thanks to Kensington H.S. holding me back, they were all one year ahead of me. Most of them asked me why I was still a freshman while they were sophomores. I tried to be truthful, but that brought either disbelief and surprise, or wise remarks. Some suggested that it was OK to start in Buffalo, but now I should get with it and come to Chicago, Brooklyn, or Boston.

After the Jamboree, the Brooklyn crowd came to James Street. Mother prepared dinner for us. She made soup using five cans of Campbell's to six cans of water. That's how broke we were. Our guests slept on the floor.

The following day, as our guests were getting ready to return to Brooklyn, the drive shaft fell out of their car. It was a 1940 Cadillac. One of my friends had some background in car repair. He diagnosed the problem as minor, if, and that was a big if, we could get a certain replacement part. We called several auto junk yards and lucked out. The car was repaired, and our guests returned to Brooklyn.

Later in the summer, I took a bus trip to New York City with Spence, a pharmacy school friend. At that time there was no thruway, so the trip lasted eighteen hours. We arrived in late afternoon and checked in at the Hotel Dixie, just off Times Square. First time tourists that we were, we made a big effort to see as much as possible. We also visited my Lithuanian friends in Brooklyn. That was an experience. Kizlauskas lived on the fifth floor of a walk-up tenement. The stairs were so darn stuffy that I almost felt short of breath upon reaching the very top. A window opened to the fire escape.

One floor below us a family was having a battle royal over sleeping rights. One person claimed that it was his night to sleep on the fire escape, and the other, using very expressive language, denied it. Spence, my Buffalo friend, did not speak any Lithuanian and had no idea what the row was about. We explained. Covered with sweat himself, he did not laugh.

That was my one and only exposure to a Lithuanian immigrant ghetto. The next day we took the eighteen-hour Greyhound ride back to Buffalo.

A few weeks later, there was a beach party at the cottage of one of my classmate's parents. The cottage was located in Long Beach, Canada, one hour from Buffalo. The day was misty to the point where one did not see any shadows. It was quite humid and warm. We swam a lot and played a lot of ping-pong. There was absolutely no wind. Shortly after sundown, we gathered what was to be gathered and left for home. Helaine and I were seated next to each other. I had always liked her, and this time, emboldened by her nearness and the relative darkness, I turned her face and tried to kiss her. She gently pushed me away. I was very hurt and disappointed, and this sadness lingered with me for some time.

The next day, I could hardly wear my pants because of the sunburn at my belt line and behind my knees. My back was equally tender when touched by the shirt. That was a hard way to learn what a misty day on the beach of Lake Erie could do in late summer. Still, it had been a happy weekend, and no-one could imagine the cataclysm that would occur the following Thursday.

On August 20th, 1953, Father died of coronary thrombosis. It was the day after Mother's birthday.

Chapter Eleven

After the funeral, I told Mother that I would get a job with the Bethlehem Steel Company and put off any further education. I felt this was the only financially viable way for our family to survive. Maria's education was not a financial question at this time. She was only six years old and attended the parochial grammar school three doors away.

Mother had different ideas. She absolutely insisted that I continue my education. She took various jobs as a cleaning woman, but social security checks were the foundation of our existence and education. Though I managed to earn enough to cover tuition, Mother provided room and board. The Brazer family was supportive, both emotionally and practically. I have always been grateful to them, both for getting us to the States and their continued moral support after we arrived.

The three of us went to order the gravestone. We had to be very careful with the stone cutter as the epitaph had a Lithuanian phrase, and we did not want to see a spelling error in stone.

September in 1953 was extremely hot. I don't recall that hot a September since. This was the month I started my second year at UB. Organic chemistry and physics had to be taken in the second year. Both were five semester-hour courses. This year was a bitch. Laboratory study took up most of my afternoons. Work downtown killed the rest of the day. The evening left me just enough time to study. Saturday was a full day of work. The only leisure time I had was on Sunday.

I was also disappointed in my work at the drug store . My exposure to the prescription side of the business continued to be nil. Most of my fellow classmates worked in drugstores, and some had learned the names and appearances of a number of medications in use at that time.

Because most teacher's seated students alphabetically, I got to know Helaine better with each passing week. Her name in those days was Hegedus. Consequently, she sat next to me. We sat together through most lectures, and our laboratory stations were adjoining as well.

The School of Pharmacy and the School of Engineering were considered the toughest undergraduate departments.

I joined a professional fraternity at some point during the second year. In retrospect, this move was not very smart. You got assessed for other members' drinking. You really did not have any more fun than those who were smart enough to not join. At that time I was basically a non-drinker, whereas some of my fraternity brothers had DWI convictions. The fraternity had been founded by the first dean of the School and was considered "the" organization to join. However, at the time of this writing the fraternity has been defunct for some thirty years.

As Helaine and I got to know each other better and better, we started to date. Eventually, we were pinned. In those days this relationship was considered more of a commitment than just going steady. She worked at a South Buffalo pharmacy in a clerk's position similar to my own. We spent many a Sunday together studying at her parents' home in Woodlawn.

It was an unforgettable school year for both of us. The first semester I aced both physics and organic chemistry. So I was very laid back, especially about physics. When the second semester finals were just around the corner, however, I realized that I might flunk the course. Cramming is the best way to describe my last week before the finals. I was sweating blood. The exam came and went, and I had no feeling as to where I stood. Finally, the list appeared on the departmental bulletin board. And there, next to my confidential ID number, was a C. I had never been so happy to get a C in my entire scholastic career. In my academic life I was never satisfied with a mediocre performance. A so-called gentleman's C was not acceptable.

Helaine went into the same exam with the following comment from her physics instructor: "Miss Hegedus, there is no way you can pass the course unless you get an A on the final." Well, Miss Hegedus got an A.

While I was a college boy, Mother was cleaning for the wealthier people of Buffalo. From her description of some of them we knew she was working for moneyed peasantry. There were some notable exceptions. Mother was a char woman for a physician, a Dr. Johnson, who was, and always remained, interested in our family. He called my Mother by her first name, Valerie. His interest lasted right up until I became a physician myself. Shortly after my internship, Dr. Johnson died.

Despite our financial difficulties, I had a car during most of my sophomore year. Father had bought an old Chrysler from a Lithuanian acquaintance in Niagara Falls. It price: $160.00. It was a 1941 model showing its age in both appearance and performance. When Father died, Mr. Grudzinskas, who sold us the car, forgave Mother the outstanding debt on the vehicle.

The car was really breaking down and required constant attention. I did repairs that could be done by an individual with no mechanical training. For example, the left front seat was supported by a piece of two by four.

Eventually, there came a time when the liability insurance was raised to $134.00. That was the end of my motoring days. I surrendered the plates, and the car was sold to a junk car dealer for twenty dollars. It was amazing that the old Chrysler even started after being completely idle for half of the winter and covered with a foot of snow.

The semester was winding down, and summer hours at the drug store lay ahead. What kind of summer was this going to be? It could not possibly be worse than the last.

Well, it was more of the same. My employers were still buying out-dated stock from long-closed drug stores, relabeling it, and selling to their own customers. These transactions probably produced a minimal profit, but my "tycoon" bosses felt that a few nickels were worth the reprehensible and unethical enterprise. Also, I was again given no exposure to any professional activities, and I wasn't allowed to fill prescriptions. I did, however, get to paint some shelves. While my classmates gained apothecary experience, I continued to wait on customers.

I recall one particularly obnoxious lunch time customer who worked at a nearby bank. His position was just a little higher than a teller, but the little man would come in and imperiously order, "Chocolate milkshake, kid!" Then he would slurp up the drink, buy the cheapest cigar in the house, and stroll out onto Main Street. This would go on day after day.

I must insert here what happened in the not too distant future. I was already in practice and had occasion to go to that bank to transact some business. The chocolate-milkshake-and-cheap-cigar connoisseur walked up to me and referred to me as "Al." This infuriated me. I lost my breeding and informed him that I did not wish to be called by my first name by a nickel cigar connoisseur. He immediately referred to me as Dr. Gamziukas. At the same time, I realized that I had allowed myself to get down to his level. The satisfaction of putting him in his place was tainted by my reprehensible manners.

Towards the end of the second semester, Mother, Maria, and I made a trip to Chicago. It was a nice weekend. We met many people from the Haunstetten DP camp. It was fun to reminisce and go over what had happened since. Because it was Holy Week, I got to see many friends from the University of Illinois at Urbana. They were home for the Easter holidays. They would all be finishing their studies in a few months while I, thanks to the reasons previously stated, would only be finishing my third year.

The visit in Chicago ended in much too short a time. It was a pleasure to be in neighborhoods where Lithuanian was spoken in stores, garages, and saloons. These thoughts went through my mind as I returned home. Particularly depressing was the fact that there were only thirty-nine Lithuanians living in Buffalo.

When I returned, I found a letter from the naturalization service announcing that on 5-5-55 I was going to become a U.S. citizen. This date became unforgettable to me. Not because its Cinco de Mayo, and not because I became US citizen on that day, but because when I returned from the Federal Court, Miss Brown, the Dean's secretary, informed me that Dean Lemon wanted to see me immediately! I knew I had missed a pharmacognosy exam earlier that morning while the Judge was ministering to us. This was particularly serious because the Dean himself taught the course.

I reported to the Dean's office. A dark cloud of foreboding hovered over me. The Dean began our interview by asking me if I felt that taking the exam was not a very important undertaking. I gave the obvious answer and explained my morning activities. The Dean then assured me that in his forty years in academia he thought he had heard every possible excuse. This, however, was a new one. Clearly I was in trouble. I told him, "Dean Lemon, I can go back downtown and ask the court clerk for an official attestation of events in the Federal Court this morning. I will not receive the citizenship papers for another two or three weeks." The Dean sat there for what seemed to me like an eternity. He then said, "I believe you. Congratulations! You were carrying an 'A' in the course; you also got an 'A' on the exam." I felt like a huge boulder rolled off my chest. This proceeding in the Dean's office was much more impressive than the proceeding at the Court.

The academic year was coming to an end. My thinking was leaning toward post-graduate education at the medical school across the campus.

The last year in the school of pharmacy was less impressive than any of the previous ones. The "401" courses were not easy, but three years of handling a 25% higher than normal academic credit hour load made all of us academic alley cats. No one flunked out in the last year, and everyone eventually passed the three day York State Board exam.

I submitted an application to the medical school. I applied only to UB. I had no money to go to an even more prestigious school. Living at home and working as a pharmacist while I studied was the only realistic avenue.

The interview to get in was more interesting than challenging. The questions I was asked did not require the brain of Nobel laureate to answer. One of the admissions committee inquired about the title of the last book I had read. I had been interested in WW II since high school; the last book I read was "Rommel's Papers". The admission committee member then asked me to compare Rommel to Patton. This was like asking me to compare a race horse to a mule. The very absurdity of the question made me immediately realize that the inquisitor was way over his head. I did not simply give an answer; I gave a dissertation. There were no further questions. Two days later a letter from the School informed me that I had been accepted. Since no one else was home, I called Helaine's mother. She was the very first person to hear my good news.

This was one of the most memorable pleasant moments in my life. The school requested a one-hundred dollar deposit within a week. It was a hell of a lot of money, but I had the required amount.

The last semester in pharmacy school continued without any surprises or special challenges. May rolled around, as did commencement. This was my first exposure to a commencement address. It was boring beyond description. Three words describe it most succinctly: multitudes of platitudes. Four years later I would attend my medical school commencement. Now I know that even the subjects of these homilies were forgotten within days, if indeed anyone paid serious attention to them to begin with.

That summer I got a job with another pharmacy. The winter before, on the second of January, 1956, I had been unexpectedly fired from my old job. I had picked up my coat and left without a word. I knew that parting one way or another was in the cards because I was still not allowed behind the prescription counter.

I never figured out why I was fired. Many years later, Helaine speculated that I could have seen some sort of manipulation of cash forbidden by the I.R.S. This could have happened! Those who were screwing the public by peddling outdated medications would certainly not be above screwing the United States government.

The summer was very hot, and I was unfortunate enough to work in the drug store of a man who thought air conditioning was an unnecessary, expensive extravagance! So was a Christmas bonus and giving any raises. Well, we all live within our own value system. However, I must say this for the boss: he was always pleasant, and as long as I performed as expected he left me alone in discharging my duties. And he put me behind the prescription counter!

Chapter Twelve

Summer rolled by, and the first day of medical school arrived. I sat in Capen Hall and listened to Dr John Warfel, who because of his avuncular personality was named Uncle John, give a lecture on the dos and don'ts of that hallowed institution. "You will always wear a necktie and a lab coat," he said, "I don't care if you call any member of the faculty Hank, Frank or Sam while at the Palace (a local strip joint). Here you will always call them by their academic prefix: Doctor. Any questions? Oh, do we have any Joe Colleges in this class? If so, you got in here by mistake. Just forget being Joe College if you want to become a physician. Now, to kill any rumors. There are eighty of you here; the school has room for you all and expects to graduate eighty physicians. Gentlemen, I wish you success." Nice speech. He was completely oblivious of the fact that there were five women in the class.

Uncle John was an impeccable dresser. His suits were always beautifully tailored. His silk ties were of a variety that I couldn't even afford. Years later, when I was having custom tailors make my suits, I meant to ask him who his tailor was, but I somehow never got to do it.

Classes started the next day. I found that I could not afford embryology or histology textbooks. I had no microscope. The professor of the two courses "leased" me a brass microscope. It looked like something out of Louis Pasteur's lab, but it served its purpose.

As I looked over the lab, I saw that some classmates had binocular Leica scopes! The damn things cost more than an entire year's tuition and books at this school. An old saying goes: the most important part of a microscope is the brain above it. How true. One of the owners of a binocular Leica flunked out during the first semester.

During the second day of classes, we had to form our own groups of four before going into dissection lab. After we were inside, each group was assigned a dissection table. Each group had to take a gurney, go into the cadaver storage room, and bring a body to the dissection table. The storage room had grey walls and was poorly lit, in order to minimize the heat in the room. I thought that cadavers would be in morgue-like "filing cabinets". They were not. They hung by the ice tongs inserted into their ears. When a gurney hit a body it created a domino effect, and all the other bodies started swinging. The atmosphere was saturated with the odor of embalming fluid. One of our group said, "This could be a good set for a TV horror show. Welcome, these are our guests for tonight!" Well, our group had no problems, even though the only place they had seen a dead body before was at a funeral parlor. That was not the case with everyone. A guy in another group passed out, and two others simply finished their medical career by going downstairs to administration and asking for their tuition money back.

After all the bodies were on the dissection tables, Uncle John gave another brief lecture. These were days when someone was cutting up at one of the New York City med schools. For example, the joker gave a toll taker a quarter glued to a cadaver's hand. The toll taker got both the coin and the hand. I bet that made his day. Another incident happened on the subway. An enterprising student glued a cadaver hand to a hanging strap. These were obviously not just pranks, but manifestations of a deranged mentality. Those students needed to be prevented from becoming physicians, at any cost.

Uncle John did not mince words. He said, "You will be given a bag of human bones which you may take out of the lab for study purposes. Yes, you may take them to study at home. Any other part of a cadaver removed from the lab will result in your instant dismissal from The School, with no opportunity to appeal. Are there any questions?" There were no questions.

And so my medical education began. The time commitment was intense. I spent hours at various labs at school. When I got home, I spent all my free time reading volumes of books.

The dissection lab affected us physically. The skin of the hands became velvety smooth. "Like the skin of a kept woman," the class comedian proclaimed. No matter how long I scrubbed after dissection, the odor of the embalming fluid was always with me. The other two labs were clean. They had no unusual odor, and they caused no dermatologic changes.

After twenty-two weeks of gross anatomy, histology, and embryology were over, I was inducted into the Gibson Anatomical Society. That was an attestation of my performance in anatomical sciences. This surprised the hell out of me. I was not particularly fond of the subjects. O.P. Jones, professor and head of the Department of Anatomy, said to me during an interview, "You must be interested in the anatomical sciences." I kept my mouth shut. To us, O.P. Jones was God's older brother.

I remember cramming at home and thinking of my pharmacy school colleagues. They now had nice jobs and did not have to worry about studying and passing exams. Well, I also had a "nice job". After school, that is.

Life entered a very busy cycle. I had lectures and labs all day. After classes I worked at the pharmacy until 11 p.m. Then I went home and studied. Some days I went directly home, and the entire evening was dedicated to the books.

Helaine was a graduate student at the School of Pharmacy. We had gotten engaged before I had been accepted at medical school, but we hadn't set a date for the wedding. I felt that it would be wise to put the first two years of school behind us before undertaking such a great change in our lives. After all, the upper classmen said that if you made it through the first two years you would graduate, unless you were some kind of screwball or misfit. I felt very strongly that I did not meet the criteria for either category.

I had purchased the engagement ring in a pawn shop located three doors away from my former employers. I had known the pawn broker for five years. He was a decent sort of a guy and very helpful in selecting a ring I could afford.

I passed the pharmacy boards and received my New York license to practice pharmacy. My pay went up only from a buck an hour to two. My boss was so tight he still had his Communion money.

Fortunately, another pharmacist told me that the owner of Ideal Pharmacy was looking for someone with my qualifications. I got on a bus and presented myself to one Cornelius Walsh, the owner of the establishment. He conducted a short interview with me. When we were done, he informed me that he would let me know. I went home, had dinner (which Mother provided for free, along with a room), and took a short nap. The bedside telephone woke me up. Walsh was on the other end; he informed me that I was hired at $2.75 an hour. That was the best waking up in my life. Going from $2 to $2.75 allowed me to pay tuition, buy necessary textbooks, and have discretionary funds left over.

At one point during anatomy dissection lab, a distinguished looking gentleman walked to our table and asked, "Which one of you is Gamziukas?" I stepped forward, wondering what kind of trouble I was in. "You went to UB pharmacy school?" I answered affirmatively. "You belonged to the Beta Phi Sigma?" "Yes, sir," I replied. What was this all about? Had my undergraduate escapades come back to haunt me? I was not a Barracuda, the Olympic drinking team of the fraternity. I had never been busted for any hell raising. So what the devil was this all about?

"Beta Phi Sigmas join Nu Sigma Nu in Medical school," he said. He wished me all the best and left. My dissection partners laughed; they told me that I had just gotten my marching orders. They implied that joining NSN would be to my advantage, but not joining would place me on terra incognita. To make a long story short, before the school year was over I was initiated into the frat of the obstetrics and gynecology professor. He was also a pharmacist and had been a fraternity brother in Beta Phi Sigma.

Months went by. Anatomical sciences were finished. The class was now into physiology and biochemistry. I had taken both subjects in pharmacy school, so the going was much easier. I even got along well with a senile professor of biochemistry who was known to demand that a student repeat a whole year, or even dismiss a student from school, just because the old prof felt offended by the student. The teacher's name is not important, but he was better known to us as "alpha D glucose". Life has since taught me that medical school attracts the extreme fringe of students, as well as professors.

The first year ended with two women dropping out. In those days one F or two D's ended your medical career. It was my understanding that the two left because of their grades.

That summer, with school behind me, I started working twelve hours a day at Ideal Pharmacy on Lovejoy. The boss was one hell of a nice guy and easy to work for. As long as the pharmacy functioned without any problems, there were no questions asked. My helpers were college age. One attended a local Jesuit college. The other attended my alma mater, the Pharmacy School.

The latter took ten years to get his degree. First, he flunked out. He had some growing up to do. Then he applied for reinstatement, but before he got in he was picked up by the local draft board for two years of military service. After soldiering for two years, he again applied for reinstatement. One had to give him credit for persistence. This time he made it! After a total of ten years, he became a registered pharmacist. I got him a case of scotch to celebrate the occasion. Most lamentably, he developed leukemia and died several years after his graduation. I have never forgotten him or the rest of the crew of Ideal Pharmacy of the late fifties.

The second year began several weeks after the freshmen class started dissecting their cadavers. Second year had one giveaway subject for me: pharmacology. I had studied this subject intensively for an entire year at the pharmacy school; therefore, in med school I got a B without really studying.

Pathology was a different ball of wax. The Professor was a Romanian German who still had an atrocious accent even after living for years in the States. One day he stood in front of the class, rocked on his feet, and announced, "Today ve vill discuss ulza." The student next to me immediately inquired, "You speak German. What the hell is ulza?" I had to admit that I did not have the vaguest idea. In my head I went through various English words and tried to match them to this exceptionally thick accent. I had no success. At this point, the professor took a piece of chalk and drew an outline of the stomach on the black board. My mental circuitry went into action, and I realized that his subject for that morning would be the ulcer!

This professor was a brilliant pathologist, his accent notwithstanding. We heard an interesting story about him. A few years before we became his students, he had been an expert witness in some ongoing trial. The opposing attorney asked him if he was Board certified in the specialty of pathology. He answered, "No." The attorney further queried if the professor had ever taken the Board exam, to which he received another negative answer. Smelling victory, the attorney continued, "Were you concerned that you would not pass the exam?" "No," replied the professor. "You see, I am a member of the Board, and I make out the exam." The courtroom erupted in loud laughter, and the judge had to pound his gavel and shout, "Order! Order in the courtroom!" The attorney's attempt to discredit the witness had been blown out of the water. There were no further questions along these lines.

The course in pathology had a weekly "viscerama". Organs from the previous day's autopsies were brought from the hospital to the School on Bailey Avenue and shown to students. I had neither a positive nor negative impression of these proceedings. The prosector, however, was a funny duck. He was obsessively meticulous. One day he spent an hour talking about the prostate of a guy, a member of the local gun and knife society, who had had his head blown off by a .45 caliber slug. I learned a hell of a lot of what happens to the prostate when a .45 caliber slug explodes the head.

Not a damn thing.

At the end of second year came part one of the National Board of Medicine examinations. Passing it was a cardinal requirement for promotion to the junior year. It was nothing to be taken lightly. As the test drew closer, a few students were told that they would take the examination in August, rather than with the rest of the class in April. This group was, in effect, being told that they were on shaky academic ground and would have to spend the summer preparing for the August encounter with the Board. Well, the entire class passed the exam, and in September everyone reported to their assigned teaching hospitals for clinical instruction.

On August 16, 1958, Helaine and I got married. It was a warm late-summer Buffalo day. The church was on Route five in Woodlawn. The Lake was visible in the distance. The appearance of the sky over Lake Erie promised a beautiful day. The ceremony started punctually, ensuring that the reception would also start on time. Festivities were held at Club Como in the South Park-Bailey area. As the wedding motorcade made its way from Lakeshore Road, it got noticeably warmer. I started to perspire, but before my shirt was saturated with sweat we thankfully walked into the coolness of the air-conditioned hall. An eight-piece orchestra was playing, and our champagne fountain was already surrounded by a group of well-wishers. In those days, many banquet halls were not yet cooled!

Helaine looked fresh and alluring. Her beauty was not wilted by the heat of the day. To this day, her wedding portrait hangs on the wall directly in front of me. Every time I sit down to work at the computer, there is the beautiful reminder of that lovely, lovely day.

We spent a week-long honeymoon in the Poconos. The Pennsylvania Mountains were a poor couple's cruise around the world. Our somewhat shaky fiscal position did not detract from the happiness of our first week together.

When we returned, we moved into a small apartment in Blasdell. The following day we reported for work at our respective drugstores. Helaine returned to Blasdell Pharmacy, and I returned to The Ideal on Lovejoy Street.

Many years later, when Helaine's parents, Paul and Charlotte Hegedus, moved, we found a paid bill for the reception among various documents. It reflected the fact that in those days people did not drink any wine, very little vodka, and even less scotch. Rye was the main spirit for perking up one's spirits. The total cost of the reception came to $937.00.

My third year at school began. I reported to the Meyer Hospital, while others reported to the General. A smaller group started with pediatrics at Children's Hospital.

As time went on, some students at the top of the class found themselves closer to the bottom. The majority, however, remained in their relative percentiles. To some, the transfer from book to bed was a huge chasm.

I drew surgical service first. This quickly made such a negative impression that selling used cars looked like a more acceptable field of endeavor. It was not the blood; it was the surgical attitude toward the patient and the world.

I realize now, from the vantage of many years of practice, that my views of surgeons and their profession were unrealistically negative. To this day, however, I know that if a choice had been presented to me of either taking up surgery or leaving medicine, I would have gotten a Ph.D. in pharmacology and forgotten about being a healer.

Surgery at the old Meyer Hospital was ruled, and I mean ruled, by an individual who came from Harvard. Initially, he worked at the now non-existent Deaconess Hospital. I interned there. Once, over a cup of coffee, the chief of anesthesia and I were discussing surgery at the Meyer. The anesthesiologist, who had a wealth of experience in his specialty and an uncanny ability to size an individual up, remembered the professor of surgery from when had done some cases at the Deaconess. The anesthesiologist remarked, "I hope he improved since he was last here."

Improved or not, the professor's idea of running a department was that of an absolute autocrat. He had a Praetorian Guard of salaried surgeons. They were of various ranks and had even more varied abilities. They never failed to parrot his dictates and show extreme deference to him. Several were exceptional teachers. Two of the chief residents were helpful and good instructors. One of them had to do another year in addition to the usual five. One autumn morning in the middle of the fifth year, while watching the resident in question perform a gastrectomy, the professor had said, enunciating the sentence in his inimitable southern drawl, "Doctor, ah think you need another year." The poor guy died of an acute coronary very soon after finishing his travails at the Meyer.

Weeks went by. One morning, a surgical resident, who I think had a particular dislike for med students who had no surgical interest, stopped me and asked if I felt morning surgical rounds were an option. My slightly "get lost" answer was phrased as, "No, but today is my first day on the medical service."

'C' building at the Meyer was the middle pavilion of the three- pavilion hospital complex. It was occupied by patients of the department of medicine. The west end of the pavilion had solaria on all three floors. Its first floor was occupied by men with a primary diagnosis of active tuberculosis.

My first morning on the service, I found myself in the nursing station. A nurse handed me a list of names and showed me a cart loaded with test tubes, syringes, and needles. She said, "You put on a gown and a mask and start in the last ward on the left." Then, as an afterthought, she added, "It's a positive ward." *Positive what?* I thought. Being completely green, I asked her what that meant. "Their sputum contains red snappers," was the answer. At this stage of the game I already knew what "red snappers" meant. Mycobacterium tuberculosis, the Tb bug. I had visions of the air being slightly pink. Visions of me inhaling this air. "Do you need help, doctor?" one of the nurses at the nursing station asked. "No, thank you," was my somewhat shaky response. Clinical clerks (medical students) were called "doctor", as well as a few other names which best not be printed.

I walked into an eight bed ward. I was going to start with a patient in a bed adjoining the windows. At the moment, no one was coughing. "Good, let's keep it that way," I thought. I approached Willie, a cheerful, pleasant black man about my age. "Y'all gonna take mah blood today?" he inquired. *I hope so,* I thought. He had veins like sewer pipes. Under other circumstances, like not in a Tb ward, this would be a piece of cake.

On the second try the needle entered his vein, and he went into severe paroxysm of cough. Cold sweat appeared on my forehead. *By Christmas I will be a patient in this ward!* What a thought to have on the first day of medical service.

Well, I did not come down with tuberculosis; however, as my rotation in the department of medicine continued, I developed symptoms of just about everything else in the medical textbook. The service was intense, requiring much effort and time. But it was interesting.

Because there was no night duty at the Meyer, I worked at the Ideal pharmacy almost every evening until it closed at ten o'clock. The pharmacy was busy at all times. The neighborhood had some eight general practitioners with frequent evening hours. The flow of prescriptions to be filled was continuous.

After a weekend in the drug store, I returned to my Tb "positive" world. I found Willie's bed to be empty. Did he die? The RN informed me that Willie would probably be back that day. I asked, "Where the hell is he?" The nurse replied, "He goes out the window most Fridays, spends the weekend with his pals, and returns." I had no idea then, nor do I now, where civil rights come in versus the rights of the public. For the ACLU I suppose the rights of an individual who has pneumonic plague supercede those of the public, unless of course only the ACLU was exposed to the plague.

The professor of Medicine was a physician's physician. He was a perfect gentleman with both the student and the attendings. His reputation was widely known in Western New York. His teaching method was strict and demanded complete commitment to medicine. In my last year, I had the privilege of spending a month with him as my senior elective. I learned more medicine during the course of that month than any other three or four months in school.

The professor's main teaching venue was a noon conference held on a different ward every day. He would ask for comment from everyone present, from the lowest house officers on up. First the interns spoke, then the junior residents, and finally, after most things had been said about the presented patient, the senior residents and the chief. Only after the trainees finished did the professor start his discussion. We paid attention to every word. Pearls of wisdom were being showered on us. No-one wanted to mess up. The professor had a temper, and he did not hesitate to show it when a patient suffered because of someone's stupidity or negligence. These conferences were my foundation for the practice of medicine. I built on it all through my career

The professor sometimes seemed ruthless. Once, a resident was presenting a case at the weekly mortality rounds. This particular individual was prone to presenting the case for longer than was required. As a result, the professor had much more time than usual to peruse the patient's chart and read the fine print. He found fault with the care, got up from his chair, and pronounced that the case had been undiagnosed, neglected, and generally mismanaged. Then, as he stormed through the door, he handed the chart to one of the attendings and told him to teach that resident how to use digitalis. To a doctor this was the equivalent of teaching someone to walk and chew gum at the same time.

The old Meyer was at one time called The City Hospital. It was built somewhere around the end of WWI and reflected the hospital architecture and logistical structure of those days. By the time I arrived there as a student, it was way past being obsolescent. It was obsolete. Outpatient clinics were in the basement, as was the x-ray department and pharmacy. The lecture hall was at the farthest end of the maze of corridors in the basement, not too far from the Tb lab and the morgue. The Tb lab closed at 4:30 p.m. The morgue and the department of pathology closed at 4:30 p.m. as well, though they would open during the night if the need arose.

This set-up caused problems for the staff and patients.

On Monday afternoons, seniors had a dermatology demonstration and lecture in the old lecture hall. Patients were wheeled into the room, and students examined them and made a presentation to the instructors in dermatology. The gurneys or wheelchairs were then removed from the hall, and orderlies would return the patients to their respective wards.

On a midwinter morning, students and instructors filed past a patient on a gurney as they exited the lecture hall. No one paid any attention to the patient, and the patient ended up being left there overnight! To add insult to injury, by the time he was found and returned to his ward the next morning, a new patient had been admitted to his bed.

The 'H' building was dedicated to the psychiatric care The fourth floor was lodgings for the night and weekend house staff. It also contained the ping-pong table. The lower three floors were devoted to patient care. The third floor was for new, usually overnight, admissions.

Our class was spread out through the entire facility. On the third floor we got to meet individuals we had seen earlier on the T.V. news. There were times we felt some of the new admissions were really dangerous; other times we felt that new admissions had been wrongfully admitted to the psycho ward.

I recall meeting a sweet fifteen year old girl. She answered all the initial psych evaluation questions as normally as you and I would. She was a picture of mental stability and social propriety. "Why is she here?" I asked the nurse, after she unlocked the door and let me out of the confines of the mental ward. "She took a hatchet to her aunt and uncle on Grand Island last night," the nurse responded. *That sweet young thing?* I thought. Assume nothing!

At rounds, another student presented the story of a new patient. The way the student presented the case made it seem that a perfectly normal individual had become an inpatient on a psych ward. This middle-aged gentleman had been enjoying a constitutional on a beautiful spring morning along the Ellicott creek. A police car came to a screeching halt beside him, and the cops pounced on the man, handcuffed him, and brought him to the emergency room. From there, he had been admitted to the 'H' building. My classmate reported that an initial examination had revealed no psychopathology. He further implied that this man's reputation could have become irreparably tarnished by events of the morning. The instructor carefully examined the write-up submitted by the student. "Did you ask him what he was wearing?" asked the instructor. "No," answered my classmate sheepishly. "The police report stated that the man was stark naked," said the instructor, "Except for a pair of sneakers, he did not have a stitch of clothing on him." The instructor closed the chart and asked for comments from other psychiatrists. Assume nothing!

My last service of the third year was pediatrics. Those students that were at the Meyer went to the Buffalo Children's Hospital. At that time the institution had a worldwide reputation. It was on the cutting edge of cardiac surgery and renal disease therapy. Patients came from as far away as Europe. Professors were the dynamo behind this academic and clinical center. Private pediatricians, in addition to salaried staff physicians, were our teachers. The private practitioners were the most prominent in the city. They had a wealth of experience in treating disease and caring for the mental health of the family of a sick child.

Practical pediatrics is what I was after, because by then I knew I was going to be a general practitioner. I was not the least bit interested in confining myself to a specialty. I wanted to care for the complete individual and his family. The salaried staff were good instructors; however, perhaps due to a lack of experience on the "front lines", many practical aspects of medicine escaped their grasps. One of the strictly academic instructors was a diminutive woman known as Minnie Mouse by generations of her students. She was extremely sharp, and meticulous to an exasperating degree. One morning, as we followed her on rounds, she stopped at an infant and asked each of us how many teeth it had. She asked every one in turn. No one knew. Finally, she looked at me and waited. "Four," I said. I had no idea how many teeth the little guy had, but I thought *what the hell*. The con man in me came up with an answer. "I am glad someone examined the mouth," Minnie Mouse said. I got away with this answer and scored some points with the instructor.

The chairman of the department of radiology at Children's Hospital was extremely interested in teaching. In my entire four years at school, no one else explained radiological imaging the way he did. He took a beaker, placed about a two-inch rubber tube and a piece of bone inside, and then filled the whole thing with water. Next to the beaker were the X-ray films. One had air in the rubber tube, and the other had water in the same tube. Using these simple objects he explained the nature of the radiologic image.

This professor also had a sense of humor. I have always remembered his aphorism about prescribing cortisone. "Cortisone makes a patient feel good as he walks to the autopsy table." This phrase reminds doctors to think twice about indications, dosage, and the length of therapy when using cortisone and its many derivatives. This is one of the pearls that stayed with me all through my practice.

The practice of pediatrics is limited to a young age group and the maladies that affect it. It is also concerned with ensuring that development proceeds in an optimal manner. Therefore, preventive medicine is one of its cornerstones. Be that as it may, pediatrics is also extremely important to anyone going into general practice. Pediatric specialists are normally closely associated with the university and Children's hospital or large wing of a university's general hospital. Their knowledge is, understandably, limited to the above mentioned parameters, with additional limitation of the field of practice to a specialty such as cardiology, endocrinology, etc. The following anecdote illustrates my point.

One of the full timers at the Buffalo Children's Hospital, a salaried specialist, developed chest pains. The rest of his colleagues, remembering their exposure to general medicine, suspected cardiac origins of the pain. They took a cardiogram. Unfortunately, none of them could interpret an adult cardiogram. They had to send the EKG to the Buffalo General Hospital by taxi. A phone call from the General informed the Bryant street facility that the EKG was, indeed, "hot". The individual was having a heart attack. He refused an ambulance and took a cab to the General. This is one of the dumbest decisions a physician could make. Nonetheless, he survived the cab ride and the myocardial infarction.

With the conclusion of pediatrics, the academic year was over. I went back to the drug store. While I had been in school, Helaine had been working full time at Blasdell Pharmacy. She was now earning twenty-five cents per hour more than me. Between us we were able to meet our expenses and have some discretionary funds.

That summer we went to Wasaga Beach, a place on the Georgian Bay in Canada. This was a poor man's Riviera. It was great. Helaine's aunt, uncle, and cousin, Marilee, were there as well, and they certainly added to the enjoyment of the week. After this getaway, we returned to Buffalo and life behind the prescription counter.

A classmate who had taken me sailing for the first time the previous summer kept inviting me to go again. After my first few excursions on Lake Erie, I knew that this was for me. Wind and wave became a lifelong love affair. After some eight years in practice, Helaine and I bought a 28' auxiliary sloop that we sailed on for thirty-seven years.

Work in the drug store, at my request, was from ten to ten. A twelve-hour shift was long, but I needed the money, my co-workers were young, and work was fun. These days I sometimes think that my happiest years were behind the Ideal Pharmacy RX counter.

The reason I got the twelve-hour shift was simple. My boss loved the horse tracks. He spent afternoons in Fort Erie when the tracks there were open and went to Woodbine near Toronto when there was no action nearer to home. My around the clock schedule allowed him to focus on his favorite pastime - the ponies.

He did have one very disconcerting habit. One night, I closed the store at ten p.m. Following the standard procedure, I cashed up. This meant I counted the money in the till and ensured that it checked against the amount totaled by the cash register. I was very upset when I discovered that the till was short by exactly $200.00. I recounted the day's proceeds. The cash was again short by the same exact amount. I turned off the lights, locked the door, and went home. I said nothing of this incident to Helaine, went to bed, and stayed awake all night. The bank bag with the day's cash was already in the night depository, and the matter was closed for the night. Missing cash does not enhance anyone's reputation, to say the least. I felt that I would be fired and not be able to get another job. I would be ruined as a retail pharmacist in Buffalo.

The next day, the boss stopped in at about noon. I went straight to him and described the financial discrepancy. "Oh," he said, "I took two hundred bucks out of the till before I went to the track." A huge weight rolled off my shoulders. But I did not let it go at that. "Why not put in a chit in the till when you do that," I asked him, "so that cashing out comes out correctly?" "Don't cash out," he replied, "Just put everything in the bank bag, and toss it into the night depository." I couldn't believe this. He just gave me a license to steal! In unscrupulous hands ten or twenty bucks could disappear every night with no one the wiser. My boss truly possessed a talent in assessing the character of those he trusted.

Medical residents of those days did not have the vaguest idea of the cost of the prescriptions they wrote. One time, during a very busy prescription filling period, I received a script from a patient who earlier that day had visited a clinic and seen a resident I knew. The prescription called for one hundred Chloromycetin capsules, with one to be taken four times a day. At that time the drug was very popular and cost fifty cents a capsule. That meant the prescription would cost $50.00, an amount that approached the weekly wages of many people. I called the resident and advised him to rethink his therapeutic choices before a patient punched me in the nose or called the police.

Unfortunately, this sort of thing has not been entirely eliminated from the practice of medicine, even today.

My last year in school started just before Labor Day. It had been one of the hottest summers in recent memory. Even the old timers who came into the store bitched about the heat, the likes of which they could not remember.

In those days hospitals were not air-conditioned, and General Hospital was no exception. Windows were open in the offices, corridors, and wards. Windows in the student quarters were the only hope for a cooling evening breeze.

Through one such open window, a thief got into the student quarters and made off with someone's pants. The poor student had to get a pair of scrub pants and spend the day on the medical service looking like a half-dressed something from the surgical suite. We did not think that the pants were the target. A wallet in the pants was a more likely objective. The pants were later found in the parking lot, but not the wallet.

The senior year began with OB-GYN. Obstetrics and gynecology. I knew that this service was important for two reasons. First, I was going to be a general practitioner. Second, part two of the National Board was in April. Passing the board was a requirement for graduation. I felt that it would be better to take the exam with this rotation finished, rather than while spending time in the department of OB-GYN in April.

I will always remember the first infant I delivered. It was at the Booth Memorial hospital, a Salvation Army institution for unwed mothers. One of the residents on night call collared me. We got into a cab that was waiting for us at the main entrance of the building. With all of its windows open, we made off through the sweltering night in the direction of Jefferson and Genesee.

When we got there, a nurse met us at the front door and took us directly to the delivery room (now called a birthing room). The resident informed me that I would be the obstetrician, while he would stand by and guide me. Everything went perfectly. This gave me immense satisfaction and the desire to do it again. This wouldn't happen, though, until more than a year later when I was an intern at Deaconess Hospital.

The episode at the Booth Memorial was rather subdued, despite my personal success. The unwed mother was happy and informed us all that the father would return now that the baby was born. However, the nurse's conversation with her made it quite clear that the girl was engaging in wishful thinking.

Medical service followed OB. It was quite different from working at the Meyer. Most of the patients were privately cared for, and all we got to do was histories of illness and physical examinations. The chief teaching methods of this hospital were frequent didactic lectures and demonstrations on the ward.

Private patients had their own private attending physicians. The busiest and most prominent of these were also the best teachers. They had a wealth of experience and taught us very meticulous, scientific, and practical medicine at the bedside. I recall one of the attendings saying, "Medicine is a science, but it takes art to apply it." Mother's physician was one of my teaching attendings. The man took the first cardiogram ever taken in Buffalo.

At that time it was unfashionable to go into general practice, or, as it is now called, family practice. Many residents would ask me why I wanted to be a traffic cop, meaning why did I want to be directing patients to various specialists. I did not argue with them. I knew that my chosen profession was big, broad, and interesting. When Mother's doctor asked me what I was going to do after medical school, I explained the negativity that pervaded the General Hospital house staff in regards to general practice. "Go into general practice. You're going to be a good at it," said the physician, who in his younger days had studied in Europe under Sir William Osler. A student could not get greater encouragement.

As the senior year continued, it was my student group's great misfortune to get a hematologist attending who labored under an inexplicable inferiority complex. Every damn day he would jab the house staff and students with negative and sometimes insulting remarks. My turn came also. After I had examined and presented a patient to him at morning rounds, he opened his remarks by asking me, "Have you considered being a plumber?" This was asked in front of the patient. The event occurred several months before graduation. By this time, to quote a classmate, "I would walk on hot coals to graduate." So I kept my mouth shut and filed the incident in my memory. My time would come someday.

And indeed it did. Some ten years later, I was introduced to him at a cocktail party on neutral ground; i.e., not at someone's home. He baronially informed me that he had no recollection of me. Well, I refreshed his memory. Before he could open his mouth again, I made a vague reference to his recently lost malpractice suit and expressed my profound feeling that he would make an infinitely better plumber than I. To paraphrase Jackie Gleason, "How sweet it was!"

Time was going by rather quickly. Soon we all were back at Capen Hall on Bailey Avenue taking part two of the National Board. It was not an easy exam. But my deep down feeling upon exiting the room was that I had passed it.

Soon after the exam, the professor of obstetrics stopped me in the hall and asked what I was planning to do about my military obligation. He caught me completely unawares. Way back, in my freshman undergraduate year, I had taken a draft deferment exam and passed it. Then, after I had been accepted by the med school, I had returned to the draft board and explained my situation to the lady who was holding my dossier. "Well then, we will write you when you become a doctor. Good luck," she said with a smile. With that visit I had put the military out of my mind until this encounter in the hall of General Hospital.

The professor asked if I had considered the National Guard. At that time I didn't even know what The Guard was. He proselytized. Drills were only on Monday nights, and just two weeks of active duty were required once a year. "Think about it and let me know," he said before he continued on his rounds. I certainly would think about it. I recalled the nice lady I had met at the draft board four years previously. I was running out of deferments. Military service was unavoidable and just around the corner. As a naturalized citizen, I felt it was my duty to serve the country as the law required, but I also wanted to get it over with in a manner least detrimental to starting a practice.

That very evening, when I arrived at work, my boss informed me that a general practitioner, whose scripts I had filled for several years, wanted to talk to me about a practice opportunity. His offices were just three blocks from the store, and he knew that I was about to become a physician.

He was extremely busy. I recalled one Wednesday from the previous summer. I had started eating a sandwich at about one o'clock, when pink prescriptions began arriving. This particular GP's office hours started at one o'clock, and his prescription blanks were pink. So I knew these were from him. After placing my sandwich in the refrigerator, I started filling the scripts. There were so many that I didn't finish my sandwich until five p.m.

During one of his call-in prescriptions, I expressed my interest in the practice opportunity. "Come in after office hours this evening," he said. I knew that his office hours ended at eight because they were stated on his prescription blanks. I also knew that his scripts would still be coming in until just before I was getting ready to close at ten.

The physician's waiting room was empty when I arrived at about a quarter after ten. The receptionist looked at me with that "not another one" look. I informed her that I was not a patient and that the doctor wanted to see me about a matter other than illness.

We went to his back office. He invited me to sit down as he filled a huge pipe. As he lit it he asked, "What are your plans after internship?" He came right to the point. "General practice," I replied. "How would you like to join me?" he asked. I answered without hesitation, "Well, I would like to practice in this neighborhood." He looked a little bit tired, but still full of vigor. He deferred any business discussion. This would occur halfway through the internship if I was still interested. We shook hands and parted.

When I got home, I found that Helaine had been worried. I never came home that late after work. Helaine and I sat down and discussed what had happened. She felt essentially like I did. I was going to be a GP. Lovejoy was a good area to start, especially since there would be some sort of remuneration from the start and no capital expenditures.

In the meantime, there was medical school to finish. I was on an elective with a surgeon from Lovejoy. I was with him every day for a month. Member of the staff of Deaconess Hospital; he performed surgery there and at Children's. Large primary care clientele at the office from prewar days considered him their doctor

The man started as a general practitioner before the war. Draft called him. After some time as general medical officer he served as a hospital commander in North Africa and Italy. On discharge he held the rank of lieutenant colonel. Taking advantage of the GI bill, he immediately entered a surgical residency.

He was a good and practical instructor. When the elective was finished, he shook my hand and said, "Don't ever worry about money. Just do the best job you can and the money will take care of itself."

During the course of the elective, I had decided to intern at the Deaconess. I let several of my classmates know what my plans were. Deaconess had many residencies in those days, and interns rotated through the Children's Hospital. The staff had a number of prominent Buffalo physicians. Within a short time, four other students started leaning in the Deaconess direction. In the meantime, Buffalo General had only two potential candidates.

Word of this got out to some of the professors associated with General Hospital. One morning, one of them approached me with the unnerving statement, "I hear that you are leading a group to the Deaconess." I immediately became paranoid, and my thoughts started racing. *I'm gonna get the shaft for screwing the General!* At this point in my medical school career I was ready to swear on the Bible that I had nothing to do with the organization of any group. I told the professor that I was not aware of any formed group, but that I myself was interested in the Deaconess. Indeed, it was the absolute truth that I did not form any group. I could not very well be responsible for the internship choices of my class mates. He did not pursue the conversation any farther. I decided from there on not to discuss my internship with anyone.

My very last lecture was in dermatology in that distant hall at the Meyer. "Gentlemen," the professor said, "now I will give you the most important lecture of the four years. Don't screw your nurse, don't screw your patients, and don't do abortions! This institution is finished with you. I wish you all every success." With these remarks, he picked up his notes and disappeared through the door. *O tempora, o mores!*

Finally, the school year was at an end. The entire class graduated, with the exception of the twelve attritions that had occurred during the first two years. The rest of us were going to be physicians! No! We *were* physicians! Added to this accomplishment was the fact that the UB med school was one of ten best in the country, that senior year was the most expensive of the eighty med schools in the United States and that I graduated in the top fifth of the class.

Commencement was to take place on Sunday, June 12, 1960. A further bulletin informed the class that participation in the ceremonies was a requirement for graduation, and roll call would take place prior to the procession. To me, and probably most of the class, this requirement was no big deal. To one classmate, however, it was a very big deal. He was a Japanese Hawaiian. He hadn't been home since he had left for Buffalo in the fall of 1956. The guy had to work, in addition to getting some family support, in order to pay for all four years. He simply had had no time or money to visit Hawaii during the intervening summers. He would start his internship, like the rest of us, on the first of July. The time between graduation and the start of his internship was just enough to allow him a worthwhile visit home in Hawaii. He went to the school administration where special consideration was denied him. He participated in commencement and met the idiotic requirement. After he finished the OB-GYN residency, he never set foot in Buffalo again.

Commencement was blessed with magnificent weather and damned with a soporific speaker. I have no recollection of who the orator was or what the oration was about. It must have been very inspiring. What truly *was* impressive and inspiring was the Hippocratic Oath. When I first arrived in America, I could never have guessed that eleven years after getting off the *General R.L. Howze* in New York harbor I would be giving this ancient Oath. As my life and practice of medicine went on, I considered the Oath almost on the same level as the Ten Commandments.

Chapter Thirteen

I returned to work the Monday after commencement. I was still at the Ideal Pharmacy. My internship was several weeks away. At this point, the Ideal was the only drugstore in town that had a pharmacist with an M.D. degree counting pills.

After the dust of graduation settled down, I decided to sign up with the National Guard at the Masten Street armory. I reported to the headquarters of the 127th Medium Tank Battalion and was given a sheaf of forms . I filled them out to the best of my ability.

One form had to do with security. It was a full page listing various organizations. Some of them I readily recognized. These were communist or communist front organizations such as the Lincoln Brigade. This brigade consisted of American communists and American idiots who looked at the world through the glasses of misguided idealism and ignorance. Many of these people fought on the communist side in the Spanish civil war back in the thirties.

After I filled out the forms, I was photographed and fingerprinted. One of the full time employees explained that I would be called if the Army found all the paperwork to be in order. About ten days later I returned to the armory, where I was commissioned first lieutenant in Medical Corps NYARNG (New York Army National Guard). I became an assistant battalion surgeon.

That same day, the people at the armory informed me that my active duty training would be held during the last week of June and first week of July.

The only acceptable reason for not showing up was death. My own or a member of my immediate family. Beginning an internship would not hold any water as far as justifications went.

I went to the Niagara Falls Quartermaster sales and bought the required uniforms and other necessary equipment. I decided to personally present myself at the Deaconess and inform the physician in charge of interns of the reason I would not be starting with the others. The man had fulfilled his military obligation in Korea. He understood my situation and told me not to worry about it.

I inquired if I could drive my own car to Camp Drum, which is now Fort Drum, and was pleasantly surprised when the battalion clerk said, "OK." Later, I learned that driving one's own car was generally not permitted. In any event, I did not hang around for someone to change his mind. That same day, I also informed my boss that I would be playing soldier at Drum. I also told him that I would like to continue working for him part time during my internship. Intern's pay was $300.00 a month!

I worked full time during the days before I reported for duty. Helaine, now expecting our first child, also worked full time. Mother almost went into orbit when she was told that I would not be in Buffalo for Maria's grammar school graduation. Helaine and I explained to her that military scheduling does not take such personal niceties into consideration, and that my orders to go to Camp Drum did not contain an RSVP. It took some doing to convince her that I really would not be able to participate in the graduation. She was ticked off at the Guard, and at me for signing up with the battalion.

My first tour of duty was a drab affair. As soon as I arrived at Drum, I was promptly detached to a rifle battalion out of Auburn. I found out very quickly that the armory in Auburn was the center of their social universe. Being invited to a ball, especially the New Year Eve ball was living at the social pinnacle.

I was a complete outsider at the staff meetings of the 108th Armored Rifle Battalion. It was like being a non-member at some exclusive men's club. They were, however, within the structure of rank, pleasant to their temporary battalion surgeon.

The two weeks went by quickly. I got to fly in a helicopter, ride in an armored personnel carrier, enjoy life in the field, and sample Army food. Having had extensive camping experience as a scout, I found being a Medical Corps officer in the field downright enjoyable.

After the two weeks passed, I returned home and reported to Deaconess for the first day of my internship. I had some apprehension. I would have to stand on my own two feet and take the rap for my actions.

The chain of responsibility of the house staff was simple. You got a new patient, performed a H&P (history and physical), and ordered what you thought was appropriate in lab, radiology and cardiology. Cardiology in those days consisted of ordering a cardiogram. Then you called the medical or surgical resident, depending on which service you were, and went to other duties. Only the resident called the attending M.D. Other duties consisted of doing procedures particular to the clinical service, medical or surgical. These procedures were as diverse as giving medications intravenously, doing chest or abdominal taps to remove fluid, changing bandages and catheterizing men, and performing fecal disimpactions. These were known as scutt work by generations of interns. It really meant the lowest category of work that the intern was responsible for. There was a host of other procedures, such as pronouncing dead patients dead and obtaining permission for autopsy.

During the first few days of my arrival, I suggested to the other five American graduates that it would be better to work alone every third night than to work with one other intern every other night. My feeling was simply that I would rather skip one night's sleep and have two nights at home, than have less work every other night and have only one night at home. My proposal was accepted by the majority, although some of the foreign graduates, who lived at the Hospital, had some reservations. A month later, however, even they felt that two nights off in the row was a good idea.

We essentially worked about one hundred and fifteen hours a week and got $300.00 a month, which amounted to $115.00 take home pay every two weeks after taxes. Vacations? There were no vacations; however, they could not stop me from discharging my duty as an Army Reserve officer at Camp Drum. So I was not penalized by the hospital for showing up one week late. That was, and I believe still is, the law.

I think it should be mentioned that the five UB grads knew that the pay at Sisters of Charity Hospital, located down Humboldt Parkway, was $400.00 a month. That was exorbitant pay in 1960! We all felt that Sisters had upped the ante because there was something wrong with the program and their recruitment was way down. Only one member of our class had gone to intern there. To this day, after almost thirty years of practice at Sisters, I am not sure that we weren't overly paranoid. We also preferred the Deaconess because our program had a rotation through Children's Hospital. This was extremely important to someone going into general practice.

My first service was surgery, and my first assignment was the emergency room. The Deaconess ER was never very busy, but I had some interesting experiences there. The first such experience was on a slow midweek day. There were no patients in the ER. I was just shooting the breeze with the nurses. A doctor, who was known for being somewhat of an oddball, came bursting through the door asking, "Where is the patient?" Behind him were two Buffalo cops. It seems that the good doctor had been speeding, really flying, when the radar car nailed him. He got brusque with the cop and told him that he was on his way to see a critically ill patient in the Deaconess ER. The cop suspected something because he immediately told the doc that they would escort him. Siren, emergency lights, and all. It was very embarrassing when the doctor and his police escort entered a totally empty emergency room.

The custom in those days was that physicians did not charge police or firefighters for their office services. Consequently, the police extended reciprocal courtesy, unless the doc got arrogant or insulting. Such behavior was frowned upon by the entire medical community. It was felt that one boorish individual could cause damage to the unwritten, but widely accepted, practice.

The surgical rotation involved many hours spent holding retractors in the operating room and many mornings spent changing dressings. Retractors were commonly called idiot sticks because anyone, even a passerby on the street, could hold them. I had no interest in the operating room, but performed my duties without complaint because it was part of the rotating internship.

One day, to my great relief, a classmate asked me if I would be interested in swapping one month of my surgery for one month of his medicine. I could hardly believe this proposition. It was heaven sent. All the surgery I was interested in was learning how to perform superficial excisions and the repair lacerations. As a general practitioner I would limit myself only to office procedures. And because all surgical diagnosis is done outside the operating room, there was nothing for me in the operating theater beyond a review of anatomy. I readily agreed to trade rotations.

Several days later, the same individual asked me if I would be interested in another swap. This time I traded a surgical rotation for one in pediatrics.

My classmate, Charlie, was going into radiology. Ever since he had been a radiologic technician in the Navy, his dream had been to become a radiologist. Medical school and internship were just nuisances in the way of his vision. His wish was fulfilled. He became one of the outstanding radiologists in Western New York. During the length of my practice years, he performed 100% of my ambulatory x-ray imaging.

I entered medicine at the time of certain changes for the better. The city in those days was full of shingles in front of doctors' offices proclaiming this was the office of so and so, Physician and Surgeon. Reason tells us that one is either a physician or a surgeon. The unfortunate cause of this was that hospitals were giving surgical privileges to individuals who had no surgical training and the state of New York gave a license to practice "Medicine and Surgery"

At the Deaconess, like at every other hospital, there was a cadre of general practitioners with surgical privileges. These varied in quality from outstanding to dreadful. The outstanding limited themselves to that which they could perform well, and never went into areas of surgery that they recognized as being beyond their abilities.

Some of the best surgeons in the city had no formal training. They were busy, and the scope of their work was that of today's formally trained general surgeon. They attained their status by peer recognition. Peer recognition is probably the ultimate credential. Most physicians know that taking residencies in prestigious hospitals and attaining board certification may not make a doctor more than mediocre. And in medicine, as in other fields, mediocrity does not earn peer acclaim.

The governance of most American hospitals consists of the board of trustees, the administration, and the medical staff. Their influence and power is variable. For example, although the medical staff is the most authoritative body to recommend individual physician's privileges, only the board of trustees can grant them and be absolutely responsible for their actions.

When I came on as an intern in 1960, there were allegations that some ten years earlier the medical staff had voted to move the hospital to the area now occupied by the Lord Amherst hotel, close to Kensington and Main Streets in Snyder. The desire of the overwhelming majority of the medical staff, supposedly more than ninety percent, was completely disregarded by the board.

For reasons that were never entirely clear, they decided to build a new hospital at the old location. This lamentable decision prevailed, and some twenty-five years later the hospital ceased to exist. The desirable collegiality between the staff and the board simply was not there.

I found it peculiar that in this institution, as well as other hospitals, patients were not seen in a timely manner. For example, a woman was admitted for a hysterectomy. After the operation, she was returned to her hospital bed. The next day I changed her dressings. And the next day, and the next, and the next. All this time I thought that the attending surgeon was seeing her when I was not on the ward. On the sixth day of my care, she asked me where her doctor was. She made it very clear that I was the only physician that had seen her since the day of the surgery. Mine were the only progress notes in the chart. That did not necessarily mean her doctor hadn't seen her. The house staff always wrote notes; the attendings only added information when they felt it was important.

I went to the coffee shop for a midmorning coffee. There, sitting at the table with other surgeons, was my absentee surgeon. I walked up to him and asked for a private word. I explained that the lady on 3C was livid because he had not seen her postoperatively. He suggested that we see her right then. This, I thought, was going to be good. "Doctor," he said, "I will now teach you more medicine than UB did in four years."

We entered the four bed ward where Mrs. Smith (not her real name) occupied the far bed by the window. "Mrs. Smith!" the surgeon exclaimed. "What have you done to your hair? You look at least ten years younger!" He approached her bed. He clasped her right hand in both of his and told her how Dr. Gamziukas had checked on her every day and kept him informed. "Today Dr. Gamziukas told me that you are probably ready to go home." He lifted the dressing and informed her that he certainly agreed with Dr. Gamziukas' opinion.

By this time Mrs. Smith was all smiles. She was essentially eating out of his hand.

This episode reminded me of a question an elderly attending had asked of our group of students the previous year. "Which is most important?" he asked, "Ability, availability, or affability?" Well, we all answered ability. "No," he said, "affability is most important." Indeed it is.

I did not see much trauma surgery while I served in the department of surgery. I suppose that was due to the fact that the hospital was located almost in the geographic center of the city and did not participate in emergency ambulance coverage. There were no expressways anywhere near the area. Trauma cases were taken to the hospitals that formed almost a circle around Deaconess.

Surgery, of whatever specialty, was mostly elective. A patient would arrive the day before the proposed surgery. Then, after a variable number of days, barring complications, the patient would go home for recovery. I do not wish to compare surgical patient treatment today with that of the mid twentieth century. Any magazine or newspaper will fill the reader in on the major differences and relative importance of patient versus cost. I will say, however, that a patient in those days had more pre and post-operative time at the institution. Consequently, an intern had more opportunity to learn about pathophysiology and the psychology of surgical care.

Surgical procedures themselves were of no interest to me because I would never use them in my practice. Learning to recognize the host of surgical signs and symptoms, however, was of cardinal importance, especially when making a house call in the wee hours of the morning. At that point, a doctor's persona had to be both Mayo and Cleveland clinics rolled into one. The guys at the hospital had all of the institution's resources behind them, while the front-line doctor had only his little black bag. He had to be good.

The nursing staff at the hospital was exemplary. I learned a lot from them. One ex-Navy nurse in particular was a no-nonsense care provider. One night we had a post-operative patient who developed ileus. Ileus is the inability to pass gas that accumulates in the bowel post-operatively. This poor guy had to have a tube passed through his nose and into his stomach. The tube is generally called the NG (naso-gastric) tube.

Using a stethoscope we checked for bowel sounds. Complete silence. The patient had no peristalsis or contraction sounds of the bowel. Half-jokingly, I said to the nurse, "In the olden days, I guess, they would use a turpentine stupe." "Do you know what it is?" asked the nurse. I explained that I was a pharmacist before becoming an MD. We had a hurried discussion about how stupes were used and where they were applied. She asked me if I was willing to give it a shot. "What have we got to lose?" I answered, firmly enough to make her realize I was not kidding.

A stupe consisted of several layers of flannel enclosing something moist and warm to hot. Old medical texts mentioned warm turpentine. We had to go about finding these materials. Thankfully, we were both on the graveyard shift, so there were no busybodies floating around to inquire about funny odor or the search for flannel at that hour. To this day I sometimes try to fathom what another nurse or orderly would have thought if we had told them we were going to apply a stupe. Not wanting to display their ignorance, they would have probably dropped the subject or thought that we were working too hard and our trolleys were slipping the tracks.

We found some flannel in housekeeping. Then I went to the pharmacy and asked the duty pharmacist if she had some turpentine. She knew that I was also a pharmacist. I feared to think what she thought. "Gamziukas, for some reason, is not playing with a full deck tonight," was as good a bet as any. "No," she replied, "but all day long we smelled turpentine in the hall where the maintenance people were doing something."

Before she could ask what I was going to do with turpentine, I was out of the pharmacy and in the hall. There was no turpentine odor any more at this late hour. At the end of the corridor stood an eight-foot stepladder. As I got closer I saw neatly folded drop sheets and a gallon size tin can standing on the floor next to the wall. There was no label on the can. I unscrewed the cap and immediately got a whiff of terebinthinate odor. The can was half-filled with turpentine. It was rather careless of the maintenance people to leave a flammable fluid just standing in a can at the end of the corridor, but that was not our immediate concern. Mr. Holzschneider's (fictitious name) ileus was what we were trying to relieve.

Now that we had our materials, we made a huge poultice using a few teaspoons of turpentine and flannel soaked in warm water. This was applied to the patient's abdomen and covered with a blanket. The old navy reserve nurse resumed where she had left her work, and I sat down to enter our undertaking in the patient's chart. While doing the paper work, I got another call to see a patient on a different floor. After forty or so minutes, I was back making entries in the chart.

Mr. Holzschneider's room was diagonally across the hall from the chart room. The patient was visible from where I was sitting. A senior student nurse walked into the chart room and announced that the smell in the room across the hall was terrible. "Turpentine and farts," she explained. "Farts?" I asked. I went across the corridor and into the patient's room As I entered, there was a thunderous passage of flatus. I placed my stethoscope on his belly and confirmed the presence of bowel sounds. To this day I have no idea if the stupe had anything to do with it, or if he improved by himself.

Now we had to get rid of the turpentine odor. It was the middle of the autumn, but still quite warm. We opened the windows as wide as they would go, plugged in a fan generally used during the hottest part of the summer, and poured better than half of a bottle of alcohol onto the floor. The flannel was removed from the ward and disposed of outside. We certainly did not throw it into a laundry hamper.

By the time the night supervisor nurse got to our floor, the odor was pretty much gone. The floor nurse explained the entire story to her boss. She shook her head in disbelief and said that we all would have been in real hot water if the patient hadn't improved. "Don't even talk like that," I said, "You must admit it did no harm." I have related this vignette of my internship many times in various settings.

My next service was obstetrics and gynecology. The labor and delivery area of the hospital wasn't well situated. A woman in labor had to walk through a medical wing and see inside the wards, as well as smell the aroma that constitutes the ambience of a medical floor. This could be anything from the smell of cleansing fluids to bed pans waiting to be emptied. Not exactly a pleasant environment for anyone let alone a woman in labor.

Deaconess was not a big hitter in the birthing business, but it handled enough births to keep the house staff going all night. I tried to get as much hands-on experience as was humanly possible. The attendings varied in how much they allowed an intern to do. As the weeks went by, they must have sized up various interns and their abilities because they seemed to allow us to do more and more. Toward the end of this rotation, there were attendings that allowed me to perform the entire delivery.

The surgical part of the gynecology service was not inspiring. We had surgeons whose entire training had lasted only three years, and that included obstetrics. There was one surgeon that the interns called Dr. Friable Tissues. No matter who he operated on, the patient bled much more than patients of other surgeons. His technique was just not on par with the rest of the crowd. His explanation was that his patients had friable tissues.

In the delivery room, however, the same physician was a real master. Most complex cases had good outcomes when he did the delivery.

Furthermore, he was a most articulate teacher. I learned more from him than from the chief of the department.

I no longer worked as a pharmacist, not because we could not use the money, but because after putting in a day, a night, and a day of work, I was in no shape to safely fill prescriptions. One day I received a call from my former boss at the Ideal pharmacy. It was regarding an inquiry he had received from Dr. DeVincentis, the physician who had expressed interest in me as an associate. I called Dr. DeVincentis and arranged to meet with him to discuss the specifics. The meeting took place within a week. Our discussion was lengthy, but it eventually resulted in an agreement that led to my spending twenty-eight years in general practice on East Lovejoy, just three blocks from the pharmacy where I had first worked as a second year medical student.

Deaconess provided living quarters, laundry, and three meals a day, or four if one worked at night. House staff quarters were not within the hospital, but in two dwellings on Riley Street, across from the side door of the hospital. Every member of the house staff had his own room. What were once living and dining rooms were now used as a common day room. An average size TV set stood against the wall in what was the dining room. An oversize coffee table occupied the living room. This was the hub of what was called the Brown House.

Long lasting poker games made it the hub. These games would start at about noon on Saturday and continue until Monday morning. People would come and go. House staff would answer their calls and return. Attending physicians would drop in on a regular basis. Obstetricians waiting for their patients to be delivered were among the members of this club. It was mostly a quarter/half-dollar game. Over time, nobody lost their shirt nor became rich. To use a cliché, a good time was had by all. Even when I was several years into my practice, I would still drop in occasionally, for old time's sake.

The Brown House served for other undertakings as well. One evening some of us were sitting around watching a cooking show on TV. The conversation drifted to lamb shanks. A resident from Iran, whose name was Malek, suggested that his way of preparing lamb shish kabob was incomparable; it was too bad he could not demonstrate his cooking prowess. One of the Indian interns, who we called Sammy because he looked like Sammy Davis Jr., piped up. "We can do it in the bathroom," he said. "How the hell are you going to make shish kabob in the bathroom?" asked a normally phlegmatic resident. "I will make it in the ashtray stand," replied the Iranian. Well, some of us thought, it will do no harm to try.

The Iranian and I took a ride to Jefferson Avenue. In the early sixties it was a viable business area with shops of all types supported by the neighborhood people. Neither the Avenue nor the surrounding area showed any signs of blight.

We went into a small hardware store and bought a small bag of charcoal. Then we drove around until we found a butcher shop. The butcher was getting ready to close for the day. "What can I get for you?" he asked, with just a hint of a discernable accent of an unknown native language. "Sheep meat," said Malek. The butcher looked at us with a quizzical expression. I felt I should step in. "We would like some mutton," I said, in a self-important way. "You some kind of a wise guy?" the butcher asked. As humbly as I could, I explained what we wanted. The butcher looked at Malek and explained that in America it is called lamb. Malek knew what lamb was and proceeded to explain that we did not want a baby sheep; we wanted the meat of an adult sheep. I told Malek that what we would get is only called lamb; it was actually the sheep meat that he had asked for in the first place. With this confusion sorted out, Malek asked the butcher to cut the meat into cubes. The man obliged. We thanked him very much, paid for the now prepared lamb, and returned to the Brown House.

Upon our arrival, we found Sammie making skewers out of coat hangers. He had already gotten some onions from the nice lady in the hospital kitchen. The bathroom was already prepared; the window had been opened as wide as possible and the ashtray stand stood next to it. Charcoal was placed in the tray, denatured alcohol was poured over it, and the show was on the road. The smoke went very nicely out of the window.

It wasn't long before we were eating Malek's shish kabob. It was really good. New arrivals entering the Brown House immediately smelled the nice aroma of lamb cooking on the charcoal. Their first reaction was disbelief. A barbeque in an ashtray? We kept the operation going until everyone got at least a skewerful to sample. Malek had proved his point.

Unfortunately, we did not know that the window of a German intern's upstairs room was wide open. Enough smoke got into his room to wake him from his nap. With Teutonic efficiency he concluded that the building was on fire and called the fire department. We discovered this when a fire truck stopped in front of our quarters and two firemen entered the day room. They found us, in effect, *in flagrante delicto*. We got a lecture that ended with the statement that they thought doctors were supposed to be intelligent. There were no further culinary undertakings. Ever.

Several weeks after this adventure, while I worked on the wards, I got a call from Helaine. She thought she was going into labor. That was a totally new experience for both of us. She told me that her father was on his way to pick her up and take her to the General. She had become pregnant while I was still a student, and was now a patient of the professor of obstetrics. He worked only at the General and Children's.

I called the resident, who was at home near the hospital, explained the situation, and left for the General. I did not even give him time to say anything. This was not a subject for discussion. I arrived at the front door of The General before Helaine and her father. She was admitted, checked, and found to be well along in her first labor. The average first labor is about eighteen hours, but she did not take anywhere near that long. In just a few hours, we became the parents of a beautiful baby girl. She was named Lisa.

I went back to the Deaconess and resumed my duties; i.e., I fell asleep on my bed without getting undressed. About midday the paging system contacted me for an outside call. It was the OB professor's partner. I knew him from my student days as a nice, competent man who was not easily shaken up. He informed me that Helaine was doing OK and was receiving a unit of blood. My next question was about the reason for the transfusion. I knew by then that normal deliveries didn't require any transfusions. He mentioned something about blood loss. I no longer recall the exact reason he gave for administering what was at that time considered to be the most effective, most expensive and most dangerous therapy. A blood transfusion! Within two minutes of hanging up I was pulling out onto Riley Street. At the General, which was just a few minutes away, I parked the car in the lot reserved for medical students and ran to Helaine's room. She was pale, tachycardic, and looked all washed out, but there was no further bleeding.

A nurse came in the room. She recognized me from the student days. "I thought you were going to intern at the Deaconess," she said with some surprise. "I am interning at the Deaconess," I replied, confusing her more. In those days interns dressed the same at all hospitals: white bucks, white pants, and a short-sleeved, side-buttoned shirt. Only the name-tag indicated the name of the institution.

Helaine fell asleep, and I asked the RN about her condition. She said one of the sutures had torn a hemorrhoidal vein. That had started the show. Well, despite the complication, Helaine recovered from a very scary first delivery and went home at the usual time. Our life was forever drastically changed.

A few weeks later, I found myself at Children's Hospital on Bryant Street. I was assigned to the acute disease clinic, which was also known as the snake pit. That was just fine by me. Outpatient pediatrics was a GP's specialty. A GP's inpatient work usually consisted of taking care of dehydration, croup, and renal infections. Anything beyond that was turned over to a pediatric specialist, not just a primary pediatrician.

This institution, today called Women's and Children's Hospital, has been, in my view, declining since Dr. Rubin retired as the professor of pediatrics. In the late fifties and early sixties, the hospital had an international reputation. Especially, as mentioned earlier, a strong cardiac surgery program that drew patients from Europe and South America. All of that is long gone. Suffice it to say that some local pediatricians supposedly send patients to Rochester's Strong Memorial for pediatric rheumatology consults!

The snake pit had a huge waiting room. Mothers brought their entire families with them when one child was sick. Student nurses were assigned to play with, read to, and baby sit the mob of waiting kids. Mothers even brought lunches for the family because they knew that the waiting time could be many hours.

This multitude was seen by three interns and two residents. We took a chart from the pile, led the mom and child to an examining room, and proceeded to administer our healing talents. This would continue until there were no more charts in the pile. No member of the house staff could leave until all the charts and corresponding patients were attended. Sometimes we worked until seven o'clock in the evening. At this point a lonely intern would take over. He had no resident to help him. If a child was ill enough to be admitted, it was the responsibility of the intern to do all the lab work and then call the admitting resident. I recall single-handedly doing a spinal tap, performing several lab procedures on the spinal fluid, and establishing a diagnosis of meningitis. Then, and only then, I called the admitting resident.

The great majority of the kids were sick with self-limiting, garden-variety illnesses. However, good medicine requires that nothing be overlooked. Neophytes like us took much more time than a seasoned, experienced M.D. would; hence, the long waiting time. All in all I feel that we tried hard to provide, and patients did get, quality medical care. Occasionally, a pediatrician, nominally responsible that month for the clinic, would stop by, ask if there were any problems, see one patient, and disappear.

One of the full timers, who I recalled from my student days, was a real study in contrasts. For example, he had an extremely strong propensity to repeat the dictum that antibiotics or sulfa medications should never be prescribed without first obtaining cultures for bacterial studies. This meant throat swabs, urine, sputum, etc., should be cultured before using the above mentioned therapy. This was in all the textbooks and repeated again and again at rounds and lectures.

What this phony did not know was that some of the med students were pharmacists filling his prescriptions. Helaine was currently filling them, and I had done so in the past. This physician's prescriptions showed that he was prescribing sulfa and various antibiotics without obtaining the appropriate cultures. How did we know that the cultures were omitted? We asked the mother who had taken her child to see him.

On the other hand, the man had good people skills and an impeccable bedside manner. He eventually left Buffalo and went to a hospital where he attended the children of the rich and powerful.

One day, while I was laboring in the snake pit, I was noticed by a pediatrician who had attended my sister when she was only three years old. This was not our first meeting. He was my attending when I was a junior and senior med student. I had tremendous respect for this physician. Not just because of his medical expertise, but also because he came to the house once to see Maria and, when he found out I was in college, charged us only a fraction of his fee. He saw that my mother was a recent widow and we were existing on a hand to mouth basis.

In the snake pit that day, he took me aside and asked if I was interested in pediatrics. If my answer was yes, he would help me get accepted into the program. At this point, I recalled that my only A in med school was in pediatrics. I expressed my gratitude and told him that I would think it over.

Despite my success in pediatrics, I could have told him right then that I wasn't interested. My future plans had been in place for two years at that point. I just did not have the heart to tell him so.

As work in the snake pit continued, I was getting good at the diagnosis and treatment of croup, diarrhea, sore ears, and various minor rashes. I felt this service was extremely useful for a future general practitioner.

Not everything went smoothly. For example, I was not spreading the plate to the liking of the chief of clinical laboratories. Spreading the plate was a process of smearing a culture sample, from a throat swab for example, on a Petri dish. The dish's bottom contained a culture medium for bacteria to grow on.

I was called to the laboratory chief's office, where I received a stiff lecture about getting my act together. He explained and demonstrated how to properly swab the plate. I thanked him and told him that I would do my best in the future. About a week later, my last week at the Children's, I was again called to the chief's office. "Gamziukas," he said, "you are not spreading the plates the way I taught you." Then he proceeded with a long dissertation on the importance of spreading the plate his way. It became obvious that there was the right way, the wrong way, and his way. The situation was becoming a confrontation of personalities.

Keeping in mind that I was no longer a student, and that the chief possessed no power over me greater than any guy on the street, I replied,

"Doctor, by July I will be in private general practice and will no longer spread plates nor give a damn about how you would like them spread. In the office that I'm joining the spreading of plates is done by a nurse." He was taken aback by encountering such impertinence. "I thank you for your time," he said. "Good bye, Doctor," I replied. And indeed, I never again spread a plate.

The rotation ended and I returned to the Deaconess. The new building was to be opened the following day. I took my own private tour of the facility. It was impressive. There were no wards, only private and semiprivate rooms. The nurses' stations were huge, the elevator banks had large elevators, and there was tremendous lighting. It was a true example of mid-twentieth century hospital, except for one detail. It had no central air conditioning! The huge fans from the old building were now positioned by the open windows at the ends of the corridors of the new building. It was late spring, and more and more windows were being left fully open. *How is this place going to feel at the end of July?* I wondered.

Unfortunately, Deaconess was acquired by The General and stripped of much of its state of the art equipment. Eventually, it became just another nursing home. If it weren't for the interests of a power group in the fifties, the Deaconess would have become a flagship community hospital at Kensington and Main.

By then the first signs of urban decline made their appearance. For example, one late evening we were playing poker in the Brown House. By now there were no greenhorns, and the game was truly among equals. After all, a good internship teaches you things beside medicine.

While we were amusing ourselves with a deck of cards, a member of the house staff, who had a room at the back of the building, came into the day room and told us that someone was in the backyard trying to open our cars. We extinguished the lights and went to the back windows. Indeed, there was an individual of medium-height trying to pry open the window of Malek's relatively new Studebaker. It was a nice car, and Malek was very fond of it.

Someone volunteered to call the police, but Malek said, "No, we will take care of it. You go back to playing cards." He slipped out the side door with two other interns. About five or so minutes later, they returned to the card game. "What happened?" someone asked. One of the really streetwise residents squelched the conversation by asking, "What are you, a cop? Or are you writing a book?" The discussion stopped, and we resumed playing cards.

Soon, the telephone rang. The person who answered it said, "It's the ER. They need the surgical resident." Malek picked up the phone, listened for a while, and said that he would be there right away. He hung up and said, "Someone has a scalp and forehead laceration." He had a peculiar smile as he threw in his hand. After that, there were no more attempts to break into the house staff's cars.

Starting right about then, the side door of the hospital was kept locked after five in the afternoon. This quickly became a real pain. We now had to go around the building to the front door. The situation wasn't so bad when the weather was warm and dry. In the rain and after dark, however, this locking of our entrance created an inconvenience and, to some extent, danger. After the car incident, we all had the feeling that the streets around the hospital were no longer safe after dark.

This trend of urban blight continued. Eventually, it destroyed what was a nice middle-class neighborhood. Years later, I carried a gun when I went to the Deaconess after dark. I had to pull it out one time, to demonstrate that I would not be an easy mark for four would-be muggers. At that point I knew that my activities at the Deaconess would soon be curtailed. Indeed, I resigned after twelve years on the staff.

I took part three of the National Board of Medicine Examiners during the very last part of my internship. I was assigned to the Meyer Hospital. This exam was entirely bedside and conducted as follows. A patient was assigned to the candidate. The candidate then examined the patient, reviewed the chart, and presented the diagnosis and treatment plan to the proctor, who stood to one side during the entire procedure, listening and observing.

An oral examination started after leaving the ward. The proctor evaluated the candidate's activities at the bedside. Was his history taking thorough and complete? Did he do a complete and systematic physical examination? How did he relate to the patient? Did he attempt to get information illegally? Questions like "What did they say is wrong with you?" were forbidden.

Ample time was given for the exam. The patients were told that new doctors would be examining them, and that they should be completely frank with the candidates. We knew that coming up with the wrong diagnosis would not mean flunking the exam, especially if one could show one's reasoning behind an incorrect conclusion. All in all, I felt the exam was fair, and the examiner, if anything, was helpful rather than trying to make you sweat blood during the whole undertaking. As far as I know, no one who graduated from UB med school flunked this exam. While passing part two was one of the conditions for graduation, passing part three was absolutely necessary in order to get the New York state license, as well as licenses in other states. In my case, I got a California license by simply asking. New York state, slow as it is in everything but collecting taxes, did not grant me my license until the twentieth of August.

My last rotation was actually a second rotation in obstetrics, by virtue of a switch with Charlie. Monday nights were dedicated to the National Guard. One Monday, however, I was supposed to be on call in the OB department. The Guard recognized no excuses. Despite the protests of a rather lazy resident, I put on my uniform. He would have to do intern's work while I guarded the country at the armory. I told him he should be appreciative instead of complaining.

The weekly drill usually started with dinner at the officers club. It was an excellent meal that included everything from soup to desert for a buck and a half. Any cocktails one had before the dinner were priced so nominally that the officers club would be a drunk's paradise, though none of the battalion officers overindulged. I always liked these dinners as they allowed me to really get to know other officers. This made working with them in the field at Fort Drum much smoother.

My internship ended on June thirtieth. I did not participate in so-called house staff graduation. I can't remember why. It may have been another military commitment. Later, I found out that I had received an award for obtaining more postmortem consents than any other house officer. Come to think of it, I had sincerely sought autopsy permissions because of my interest in the ultimate and true causes of death. The old Latin aphorism *mortuos vivos docent* is, and always will be, true.

I was about to go into practice. But that is not entirely true. I was actually going into several years of preceptorship in the hands of my senior associate, a very sharp and experienced physician with a huge practice to support these assertions. He was also a very tolerant and good teacher.

The first of July, 1961, was a Saturday. I presented myself at 1017 E. Lovejoy, eager to begin. Doctor DeVincentis came to the back office, sat down behind his desk, lit a large pipe, and asked if I was ready. After getting an enthusiastic affirmative, he simply said, "Start in the blue room". That room was the largest in the building, had blue walls, and was the only one on the west side of the corridor. It was here that my life as a general practitioner began.

As I entered the blue room, my years of study and experience flashed before my eyes. I had started grammar school in Sirviai, continued my education in Wattens, learned German, attended a gymnasium in Augsburg, crossed the ocean, learned yet another new language, tolerated three years at Kensington H.S., became a pharmacist, sweated blood for four years in med school, and paid my dues as an intern. After all of that, I had finally come into my own.

The patient in the blue room was Mrs. Anzo, an old Italian lady who didn't speak a word of English. I introduced myself. She smiled apprehensively, but pleasantly. I took my time looking at her record. I needed to come up with a plan of action since I spoke no Italian and she spoke no English. From the rather brief entries in her record and her obviously swollen ankles, I felt she was a cardiac. She was not short of breath, her heart rate was near normal, and her lungs had only a few rales which cleared on coughing; in other words, she was pretty stable. During her previous visit, DeVincentis had given her an injection of a mercurial diuretic, the only diuretic available in those days. I also noticed that her weight and other statistics hadn't changed. I gave the same injection, wrote her prescriptions, and said goodbye.

Various dicta came to mind. The fundamental rule of medicine, *Primum non nocere* means first, do no harm. The second rule comes from the streets. If it ain't broken, don't fix it. After seeing a few more patients, I went to the back office. "Well, what do think?" asked DeVincentis. "I like it," I answered. At the end of office hours, he admitted that he had been afraid I would take a walk after the very first patient.

We started talking about malpractice insurance, workmen's compensation classification, and getting me a Drug Enforcement Administration number. All of these required that the applicant have a current, valid N.Y. State license and certification. DeVincentis concluded that working without these whistles and bells was fraught with all kinds of administrative dangers, and that I should see if anything could be done to speed up the state. A call to the Board of Regents revealed only the approximate date of licensure. A civil servant told me, "You will have your license in August."

In the meantime, the battalion was getting ready for that summer's two weeks at Fort Drum. This time we went directly to the field. A detachment was left at the armor depot to draw assigned tanks. Our maneuver area was located about half a mile from a civilian highway. The sergeant in charge of the medics advised me that the aid station should be placed along a difficult trail, as far as possible from the headquarters. There would be no real casualties, only sick calls, and the distance and difficulty of driving to it would keep snooping brass and active army inspectors away. "This guy is experienced in the ways of Fort Drum," I thought, "I had better listen to him." And so the aid tent was pitched in the middle of a small glade, while we pitched our living tents behind a stand of evergreens. A CBR (Chemical, Biologic and Radiologic, warfare alarm gong) and a Lister bag that contained potable water hung prominently beside the aid tent. A latrine was dug in an appropriate location, and signs pointing to it were placed along the path.

While back in Buffalo, I had convinced the battalion commander that if we had our own vial of tetanus toxoid there would be no need to drive anyone to the Fort hospital for such an injection. Of course, we would need a tin garbage can to hold the ice in which the vial would be kept. The colonel saw the reasoning and gave orders to the S4 officer (quartermaster) to make sure that the medics got their ice daily.

As the battalion surgeon, I had a jeep (truck - 1/4 ton, in army language) assigned to me. One of my duties was to visit each of the far flung battalion companies daily and check their latrines and kitchen facilities. One of the less pleasant duties was to sit in a makeshift ambulance on a tank ninety millimeter range for most of the day and provide what was called "medical support". Six years of doing that resulted in me needing the bilateral hearing aids that I am now wearing. The military doesn't give out a Purple Heart for losing your hearing. That's OK with me. I agree with the author of a book called "Rogue Warrior" who was very emphatic when he wrote that the idea was NOT to get the Purple Heart.

The weather that year was ideal for camping, tent living, and military training. The skies were always blue, the days were quite warm, and the nights were very comfortable. Life became quite orderly and civilized. Sick calls in the morning did not amount to more than two or three patients, some of whom where goldbricks. To add to the pleasantness, our battalion headquarters cook was a chef in an upscale Buffalo restaurant. He made army rations taste like something he would prepare back home, even as he followed the military's menu.

"War is hell," said one of the medics as he mixed martinis late in the afternoon. He got mad as hell when he found out that no one had brought any olives. The Jeep was dispatched to the town of Carthage, and the driver soon returned with a large jar of olives. Ice we had plenty of, although by that time the garbage can also contained a number of cans of beer to quench the thirst of after-duty hours. A second garbage can was "requisitioned" from the kitchen to hold only tetanus toxoid and ice. We did not want to be embarrassed by an unannounced inspection.

The medics were a fraternity. They knew how to keep their mouths shut if they wanted to have beer and martinis. For example, rumors about the medics drinking beer occasionally surfaced among the enlisted personnel at the headquarters. Whenever a medic heard such allegations, he squelched them on the spot. These confidential matters of the medical fraternity remained shrouded at least until I left the Guard in 1965.

By the time the first week was half over, I discovered from other medical officers that a certain creek meandering through the training areas contained brook trout, and at its mouth at Indian River were northern pike. I made a mental note to acquire basic fishing tackle for the following year. Then I realized that we could be in a totally different location at that time, far from these fishing areas. So I drove to Carthage and bought the necessary fishing gear. This could be a once only type of opportunity.

On my first expedition, after duty hours, I returned with 3 brook trout. We fried these, divided them as evenly as possible, and ate them while sipping a martini or a beer. As days went by, the catch increased. We all concluded that on the entire military reservation this was as ideal a location as you could get.

One day during the second week of camp, I was stationed at table VI, a ninety-millimeter moving target range. While we were on lunch break, one of the sergeants asked me if I would be interested in driving a tank. I certainly was thrilled.

In those days the standard battle tank was the M48. The number stood for its weight in tons. To drive it, one had to first start a small engine called "little Joe". This turned over the main motor. The sergeant started the engine and told me to drive. "Just like a car," he said. Well, the tank had a wheel, gas and brake pedals, and automatic transmission. Driving it cross country felt like driving a Lincoln on a paved road. The tank simply flattened any humps in its way. The great difference between a Lincoln and an M48 was that if you hit an eight-inch thick tree with a Lincoln, the car would probably be totaled and you would end up in an ambulance. If you hit a tree with the tank, you would knock down the tree, drive over it, and hardly feel the collision.

During my time on the range, I got to fire both machine guns as well as the ninety mm gun. The whole tank rocked when the main gun fired, but the noise inside the turret was benign compared to the vicious crack one heard outside.

While I was being amused with this huge toy, a head appeared in the open hatch and told us that the colonel was, "looking for the doc." I became concerned that I was going to get some sort of lecture, and the sergeant would really get into trouble. None of that happened. The colonel was pleasantly surprised that the battalion surgeon was interested in the workings of the unit to such a great degree. Since high school, I had spent a lot of my leisure reading time on the history of World War Two. Consequently, I held an interest in military things and did not have the generally negative attitude of other physicians in the Guard. Besides, I felt that a go with the flow attitude would lead to more positive outcomes in my military career. While other docs frequently asked questions that implied they knew better methods to obtain better results, I felt there was a reasonable way, a better way, and the Army way. And while in the Army, one should do as the Army orders.

I also got to meet some of the high and mighty. One morning, while standing on the Table VI range control tower with the control officer, we noticed a helicopter slowly descending towards our location. "One of the damn colonels from the division on a sight seeing tour," observed Captain Sam Zinni as he checked his paperwork, which undoubtedly the brass would want to see.

Kicking up a veritable dust storm, the chopper landed at the bottom of the control tower. Zinni picked up the microphone and gave command to the next tank to hold fast. Next, he ordered tank number six to move to position one. Then he ordered the target crew to tow the target, an old refrigerator, to the starting position. The target was towed by an electric motor along a narrow gauge track. "Sam, why are you shuffling the deck?" I asked. "Number six is Cosaniti and his men, our best crew."

At this point we both heard someone climbing the tower ladder. We looked at the gap in the railing where the ladder ended. As the man came up, we first saw the top of his helmet. It had four stars on it. This was no colonel from division. This was someone from the Pentagon.

Once the general was standing on control tower floor, Sam walked up to him, saluted, and introduced himself as captain so and so, delta company 127th medium tank battalion. The general returned his salute, introduced himself as Gen. so and so, Joint Chiefs of Staff, and shook his hand. Then he turned to me. I tried to look as military and sharp as possible. "Captain Al Gamziukas, battalion surgeon, Sir," I said. He shook my hand and remarked that he did not see many battalion surgeons in a control tower. I replied, "The ambulance is at the foot of the tower, and I can see the action better from here, Sir."

The General turned back to Sam and told him to carry on. Sam got on the microphone and told the range to proceed. The refrigerator started its run. The track was situated diagonally to position one. The longer you waited, the further the target got from position one. Cosaniti's tank fired. We could see the tracer go a little high and in front of the moving refrigerator. Within a few seconds, the tank fired again. This time the tracer knocked the refrigerator out of sight. A direct hit. "Six, move to position two," Sam ordered. The tank moved forward. Upon reaching position two, it turned right while its turret traversed to the left. Another target, this time the body of a car painted white, was making a run on a track parallel to the firing position. Cosaniti hit it with the first shot. "As good as Knox," the general said. Fort Knox in Kentucky is where the Armor School is located.

The general bid us goodbye. As the helicopter took off, Sam and I started to breathe easier. The battalion commander would be told a very good story at the evening staff meeting.

Tank ranges were interesting places. Thievery was present! Tanks would be padlocked for the night. Nonetheless, one morning a fifty caliber machine gun mount was missing from one of our tanks. We all knew that it had been swiped by a unit on an adjoining range. They had some sort of gun mount problem. The story had it that a con man from our battalion, posing as a weapons inspector, went to another range and requisitioned the mount for inspection. He then placed it in his jeep and, using a circuitous route, brought it back to our outfit.

Although Fort Drum is in upstate New York, not too far from Watertown, it sometimes has dangerous wildlife. Because of this, post rules required an armed sentry whenever there was ammunition left on the range overnight. Many people carried fire arms, but only very carefully designated people actually possessed live ammunition. A "class A agent" (payroll bearer) and an armed sentry were members of this category.

It so happened that one night our sentry was jumped by a large pack of feral dogs. These were domestic dogs that had taken to the wilderness long ago, formed a pack with other such animals, and became predatory. Our poor sentry, after expending all of his ammo, spent the night on the guard house roof. There were dead dogs all over. He was a good marksman, but he only had so many clips.

The two weeks came to an end. The tanks were power washed, checked by the regular army inspectors, and lined up for the next armored unit. The battalion formed a convoy and pulled out for the Masten Street armory in Buffalo. As we left, I thought of the obstetrics professor who had recommended that I join the National Guard. It turned out to be a very good way to fulfill my military obligation.

When I arrived home, Helaine came to meet me with Lisa, our first born. The baby started crying hysterically when she saw me in uniform. I know that army fatigues are not something one would see in Gentlemen's Quarterly, but her reaction to them was such that I had to disappear into the bedroom and change into civvies.

I had received nothing from the Board of Regents while I was away. I called Doctor DeVincentis and told him that I was back, but the license had not yet arrived. This was on a Saturday. On Monday, however, the mailman brought about another great change in my life. The mail contained my license to practice medicine and surgery.

Epilogue

I continue to live in Buffalo.

Our family was blessed with two more children, Paul in 1962 and Lynn in 1964. We became world travelers and have visited 78 countries as of this writing. Sailing became my life's other love during magnificent summers on the lower Great Lakes. I look back on a rewarding life as a physician.

I returned to visit Lithuania and the places mentioned in this memoir when the Russian occupation ended and the country became independent again. At the time of our latest visit, in 2003, the country was a member of N.A.T.O and about to become a part of the European Union. Lithuania was traveling again on the road of the society of nations belonging to the West.